CUSTOMER RELATIONS HIP MANAGEME NT (CRM)

How Succeeding Businesses Turn Prospective Clients Into Devoted Champions, Maximize Sales Using Powerful CRM Techniques, and Create the Future Of Your Company.

RICHARD N. WILLIAMS

TABLE OF CONTENTS

INTRODUCTION TO CRM

In this cutting edge universe of business, where innovation develops at a phenomenal speed, one organization stood apart as a guide of development flexibility, and extraordinary client relationship with the board. This is the tale of HorizonTech, a fair sized programming firm that turned customary way of thinking on its head, reworking the principles of CRM.

In the mid 2000s, HorizonTech wound up at a junction. The organization had delighted in moderate accomplishment as a CRM arrangements supplier, however savage contest and changing client assumptions were undermining its significance. The conventional CRM model, with its emphasis on deals and promoting, was presently sufficiently not to fulfill the steadily developing requests of the educated client base.

Rather than surrendering to the difficulties, the authority of HorizonTech chose to set out on a daring excursion of change. They understood that just overseeing client connections was at this point not adequate. The organization expected to make encounters that reverberated with clients on a more profound level, and they expected to do it in an imaginative manner.

The President, Rachel Cohen, a passionate devotee to development, revitalized her group around an intense vision. She didn't need just fulfilled clients; she needed steadfast backers who might push the organization higher than ever. HorizonTech set off to make a CRM stage that would accomplish something beyond overseeing client communications; it would give a consistent, customized venture that clients couldn't help it.

To accomplish this, HorizonTech put vigorously in innovative work. They searched out the best ability in information examination, man-made reasoning, and client experience plan. They comprehended that the core of any CRM framework is information, and they started gathering it from numerous sources, including client input, virtual entertainment, and exchange chronicles. With this information, they prepared progressed AI calculations that could expect client necessities and inclinations.

HorizonTech additionally re-imagined the client venture by transforming it into a drawing in story. Clients presently not connected with a nondescript framework; they set out on a customized experience through a virtual reality where all their means were expected and taken special care of. This change was completely exceptional.

One story that exemplified HorizonTech's imaginative soul included an entrepreneur named Bella. She had been involved with HorizonTech's CRM for quite a long time yet was attempting to extend her pastry kitchen business. At some point, she got a customized email from HorizonTech that broke down her deals information and recommended another promoting approach.

Captivated, Bella chose to check it out. With HorizonTech's direction, she began a client dependability program and started offering limits to her customary clients. In only a couple of months, her income took off, and her bread kitchen's standing bloomed. Bella's business was changed, and she turned into a dedicated promoter for HorizonTech.

Versatility was an imperative part of HorizonTech's change. The excursion wasn't without misfortunes. There were information breaks, programming bugs, and, now and again, suspicious workers. However, the organization stood tough, gaining from each test and arising more grounded. They fabricated a culture of development and consistent improvement, where representatives were urged to proceed with carefully thought out plans of action and gain from their slip-ups.

As time went on, HorizonTech's extraordinary CRM approach not just changed the manner in which organizations associated with clients yet additionally impacted different ventures. The standards of information driven personalization, expectant assistance, and client narrating began to build up forward momentum around the world. HorizonTech was at this point not simply an organization yet an impetus for change.

By 2023, HorizonTech was on the forefront of CRM innovation, and their inventive methodology had drawn worldwide recognition. Their client backing rate was among the most elevated in the business, and their clients crossed assorted areas. HorizonTech's motivating story propelled endless different organizations to reevaluate their client connections, transforming CRM into something more significant.

Eventually, HorizonTech's process was a demonstration of the force of development and flexibility notwithstanding misfortune. They didn't simply oversee client connections; they changed them. Their story advises us that in a quickly impacting world, embracing development, gaining from misfortunes, and making significant client encounters can prompt a wonderful change that contacts the hearts and brains of clients and organizations the same.

What is Customer Relationship Management?

(CRM): Supporting Client Dedication and Development

In the quick moving and profoundly cutthroat universe of business, keeping up areas of strength for clients has become principal. Client Relationship The board, generally known as CRM, is a fundamental technique and innovation that engages associations to oversee and improve their communications with clients. This diverse methodology helps with securing new clients as well as assumes an urgent part in holding existing ones.

Grasping CRM

At its center, CRM is an extensive way to deal with an organization's cooperations with its clients. It includes gathering, coordinating, and breaking down information to grasp client inclinations, ways of behaving, and needs. CRM incorporates innovation as well as the systems, cycles, and strategies that guide client connections all through their whole life cycle with a business.

Parts of CRM

Information The executives: Integral to CRM is information. Organizations gather and store a huge measure of client information, including individual subtleties, buy history, inclinations, and criticism. CRM frameworks work with the association and recovery of this data, making it available to different divisions inside the organization.

Client Obtaining: CRM distinguishes likely clients by dissecting information and focusing on unambiguous market portions. This empowers organizations to tailor their promoting endeavors and associate with the right crowd.

Client Maintenance: A huge piece of CRM is centered around continuing to exist clients fulfilled and steadfast. By understanding their inclinations, organizations can give customized encounters, which, thus, can cultivate steadfastness.

Deals Robotization: CRM programming frequently incorporates highlights for overseeing deals processes, for example, lead age, opportunity following, and deals determining. This smoothes out deals endeavors and helps in finishing on more proficiently.

**Promoting
Mechanization:** Computerized promoting efforts, email advertising, and client division are essential parts of CRM. These devices help in supporting leads and keeping in touch with clients.

Client care: CRM works with effective client assistance by offering help specialists with far reaching client data. This empowers quicker issue goals and a superior client experience.

Investigation and Revealing: Information examination is pivotal in CRM. It assists organizations with settling on educated choices and surveys the viability regarding their methodologies. It likewise gives experiences into client ways of behaving and drifts.

Integration: CRM frameworks frequently coordinate with other business apparatuses and applications, like email, web-based entertainment, and internet business stages. This guarantees a consistent progression of information and data across the association.

Advantages of CRM
Carrying out CRM offers a horde of benefits for organizations, going from little new businesses to enormous undertakings. A few key advantages include:

Further developed Client Getting it: CRM gives a 360-degree perspective on clients, permitting organizations to comprehend their inclinations and ways of behaving better. This information is important in fitting items and administrations to address client issues.

Improved Client assistance: With admittance to client information, support groups can offer customized help, settling issues all the more successfully and making a positive client assistance experience.

Expanded Deals Proficiency: Outreach groups benefit from CRM's robotization and association, which prompts improved lead the board and more limited deals cycles.

Client Maintenance and Steadfastness: By customizing collaborations and conveying what clients need, CRM helps construct long haul connections. Faithful clients are bound to make rehash buys and prescribe the organization to other people.

Information Driven Direction: CRM's investigation and announcing apparatuses offer bits of knowledge into market patterns and client ways of behaving. This data guides key choices and promotes endeavors.

Cost Decrease: CRM frameworks smooth out business tasks, diminishing manual endeavors and expanding productivity. This, thus, prompts cost investment funds.

Upper hand: Organizations with a very much carried out CRM framework frequently beat contenders by offering predominant client encounters and focusing on their promoting endeavors successfully.

The Job of CRM in Present day Business

In the present computerized age, where shoppers are immersed with choices and data, CRM has turned into a key part of business achievement. It is something beyond a device; an essential way of thinking cultivates client centricity. This is the way CRM assumes a basic part in current business:

Personalization: Present day clients request customized encounters. CRM empowers organizations to make customized promoting efforts, suggest items, and offer help in light of individual inclinations.

Omnichannel Correspondence: With CRM, organizations can keep a steady presence across different channels, be it email, web-based entertainment, or in-person corporations. This guarantees that clients can draw in with a brand in their favored way.

Client Information Security: As organizations gather and store huge measures of client information, guaranteeing its security and protection is central. CRM frameworks frequently accompany strong security highlights to safeguard delicate data.

Scalability: CRM frameworks can develop with a business, making them reasonable for the two new companies and laid out endeavors. This versatility guarantees that as an organization extends, its CRM can adjust to its evolving needs.

Upper hand: Organizations that really use CRM have an edge over contenders who are not as client centered. By utilizing information and examination, they can pursue information driven choices that put them aside on the lookout.

Variation to Change: In a quickly changing business scene, CRM assists organizations with remaining light-footed and adjusting to showcase shifts. It considers speedy changes in showcasing and deals methodologies in light of arising patterns.

Long haul Worth: CRM encourages connections that lead to client reliability and long haul esteem. Fulfilled, faithful clients are bound to make rehash buys and advocate for the brand.

Difficulties and Contemplations

While CRM offers various advantages, its execution can be challenging. Organizations should think about variables like the expense of gaining and keeping up with CRM frameworks, staff preparing, and guaranteeing information protection and security. Moreover, social changes inside the association may be expected to embrace a client driven approach completely.

Client Relationship The board isn't simply an innovation; a way of thinking places clients at the core of a business. In a period where client assumptions are higher than at any other time, CRM gives the resources to convey customized encounters, sustain dependability, and drive development.

Importance of CRM in Sales

Client Relationship The board (CRM) is an indispensable part of current deals techniques. It fills in as the foundation of organizations expecting to construct, keep up with, and improve their associations with clients. In this quickly advancing business scene, the significance of CRM in deals couldn't possibly be more significant. This article digs into why CRM is urgent for deals achievement and investigates its different features.

CRM Characterized:

CRM is a complete methodology that organizations embrace to oversee and dissect their communications with clients all through the client lifecycle. It includes the utilization of innovation, methodologies, and cycles to accumulate, store, and dissect client data. CRM isn't just about overseeing current clients yet additionally gaining new ones, as it permits organizations to all the more likely figure out their interest group and design their way to deal with their necessities.

Client Maintenance:

One of the most quick advantages of CRM in deals is its effect on client maintenance. It assists organizations with figuring out their clients on a more profound level by following their inclinations, buy history, and input. This information empowers organizations to customize their connections and give a predominant client experience. At the point when clients feel esteemed and comprehended, they are bound to remain faithful to a brand.

Expanded Effectiveness:

CRM frameworks smooth out deals processes by giving an incorporated stage to overseeing leads, contacts, and correspondence. This diminishes manual information passage, limits mistakes, and saves time, permitting outreach groups to zero in on what they excel at — selling. Besides, computerization highlights in CRM frameworks can deal with routine assignments like sending follow-up messages and booking arrangements, further supporting productivity.

Information Driven Independent direction:

In the advanced business scene, information is above all else. CRM frameworks gather and store an overflow of important information on client conduct and deals execution. This information can be tackled to come to informed conclusions about item improvement, promoting procedures, and client division. It permits organizations to adjust rapidly to changing economic situations and client inclinations.

Further developed Client Division:

CRM frameworks empower organizations to section their client base into unmistakable classifications in light of different models like socioeconomics, conduct, and inclinations. This division is priceless for making designated showcasing efforts and fitting item contributions to various client gatherings. It guarantees that assets are allotted all the more successfully, prompting higher deals and return on initial capital investment.

Personalization:

Personalization is a popular expression in the deals and showcasing world. CRM frameworks assume a vital part in this by permitting organizations to convey customized content, offers, and suggestions to individual clients. By utilizing the information put away in the CRM, organizations can create messages and offers that reverberate with every client's one of a kind requirements and inclinations.

Lead The board:

Overseeing leads is a basic part of the deals cycle. CRM frameworks help organizations track and sustain leads successfully. They give experiences into which leads are probably going to change over, empowering outreach groups to zero in their endeavors on high-likely possibilities. This, thus, builds the change rate and lifts by and large deals.

Further developed Correspondence:
CRM frameworks work with better correspondence inside outreach groups. They give an incorporated stage to sharing data about leads, possibilities, and clients. This guarantees that everybody in the group is in total agreement and can give reliable and excellent help to clients. It additionally keeps leads from escaping everyone's notice.

Anticipating and Arranging:
Exact deals estimating is significant for business arranging. CRM frameworks give verifiable deals information, which can be utilized to make figures and set sensible deals targets. This is instrumental in overseeing assets, stock, and faculty really.

Client assistance:
In the present exceptionally cutthroat market, client care is a critical differentiator. CRM frameworks assist organizations with conveying extraordinary client care by giving moment admittance to client data and history. This guarantees that client requests and issues are settled rapidly and acceptably.

Scalability:
As organizations develop, the volume of client information and deals exercises

additionally increments. CRM frameworks are profoundly versatile, making them reasonable for organizations, everything being equal. Whether you're a startup or a global company, a CRM framework can adjust to your changing necessities and oblige your growing client base.

Cost Decrease:

While executing a CRM framework can be an underlying speculation, the drawn out benefits incorporate expense decrease. Via robotizing routine assignments, taking out manual information passage mistakes, and further developing productivity, organizations can set aside cash over the long haul. CRM frameworks additionally help in diminishing client obtaining costs as they further develop lead the board and transformation rates.

Upper hand:

In the present hyper-cutthroat business climate, it is essential to remain in front of the opposition. CRM frameworks give organizations an upper hand by assisting them with understanding their clients better and give them a prevalent encounter. At the point when clients have a positive collaboration with an organization, they are bound to pick that organization over its rivals.

All in all, the significance of CRM in deals couldn't possibly be more significant. It isn't just an innovation yet an essential methodology that engages organizations to fabricate and keep up serious areas of strength for associations with their clients. From further developing client maintenance to expanding proficiency, personalization, and navigation, CRM offers many advantages that are fundamental in the present deals scene. To prevail in the dynamic and client driven market, organizations should embrace CRM as a basic piece of their deals methodology.

Chapter 1
Key
Components of
CRM

CRM is a far reaching methodology that assists organizations oversee and work on their associations with clients, eventually prompting expanded consumer loyalty, steadfastness, and business development. To accomplish these objectives, CRM includes a few key parts:

Client Information The board:
Key to CRM is the powerful administration of client information. This includes gathering, putting away, and arranging data about clients, for example, their contact subtleties, buy history, inclinations, and cooperations with the organization. This information fills in as the establishment for customized and designated showcasing and client care.

Deals Robotization:
CRM frameworks frequently incorporate deals mechanization apparatuses that smooth out and enhance the deals

cycle. These devices can aid lead the executives, opportunity following, and deals gauging. Via computerizing routine undertakings, outreach groups can zero in on building and sustaining client connections.

Showcasing Robotization:

CRM frameworks work with designated showcasing endeavors through mechanization. This incorporates email showcasing, lead supporting, and mission the board. It assists organizations with contacting the right crowd with the ideal message brilliantly, improving client commitment and change rates.

Client care and Backing:

Outstanding client care is a critical part of CRM. CRM frameworks empower organizations to follow and oversee client requests, protests, and demands effectively. They likewise support multi-channel support, permitting clients to interface through their favored correspondence channels, like telephone, email, visit, or online entertainment.

Examination and Detailing:

CRM stages offer powerful examination and revealing abilities. By breaking down client information, organizations can acquire important bits of knowledge into client conduct and inclinations. This information driven approach helps in pursuing informed choices and thinking up techniques for client commitment and maintenance.

Client Division:

Powerful CRM includes dividing clients in view of different rules, like socioeconomics, purchasing propensities, and inclinations. This permits organizations to fit their promoting and deals endeavors to various client gatherings, working on the significance of their interchanges.

Coordination with Different Frameworks:

CRM frameworks frequently coordinate with other business frameworks, like ERP (Endeavor Asset Arranging) and promoting programming. This mix guarantees the consistent progression of information among divisions and empowers an all encompassing perspective on client communications and exchanges.

Portable Access:

In the time of versatile innovation, CRM frameworks offer portable applications that empower sales reps and client care agents to get to basic client information and play out their undertakings while in a hurry. This adaptability upgrades efficiency and responsiveness.

Social CRM:

With the multiplication of virtual entertainment, organizations need to deal with their presence on these stages. Social CRM includes observing online entertainment channels for client communications, criticism, and notices, permitting organizations to answer instantly and draw in with their crowd.

Client Self-Administration:

Numerous CRM frameworks incorporate client self-administration entries, where clients can get to data, make buys, or resolve issues autonomously. This lessens the responsibility in client support groups and engages clients to track down arrangements whenever the timing is ideal.

Work process Computerization:

CRM frameworks frequently consolidate work process robotization to smooth out inner cycles. For instance, they can computerize lead task, follow-up updates, and endorsement processes, guaranteeing that assignments are executed proficiently.

Information Security and Protection:
With the rising spotlight on information security and security guidelines, CRM frameworks should integrate powerful safety efforts to safeguard client information. Consistency with regulations, for example, GDPR and CCPA is fundamental.

Scalability:
CRM frameworks ought to be versatile to oblige a developing client base and advancing business needs. Versatility guarantees that the CRM arrangement stays powerful as an organization extends.

Customization:
CRM frameworks ought to take into consideration customization to fit the stage to the particular necessities of a business. This incorporates custom fields, work processes, and reports.

Preparing and Backing:
Executing a CRM framework requires legitimate preparation and progressing support for clients. Organizations ought to put resources into preparing to guarantee that workers can augment the framework's advantages.

Input and Persistent Improvement:
Consistently gathering and examining criticism from clients and workers is essential for further developing CRM methodologies. Adjusting to changing client needs and economic situations is

fundamental for the drawn out progress of a CRM program.

All in all, CRM is a complex methodology that envelops different key parts to further develop client connections and drive business development. Successful CRM includes overseeing client information, mechanizing deals and promoting processes, giving uncommon client care, and utilizing investigation and detailing. It additionally incorporates components like client division, mix with different frameworks, and consistency with information security and protection guidelines. By executing and improving these CRM parts, organizations can upgrade consumer loyalty, faithfulness, and generally speaking achievement.

Customer Data Management and Sales Automation

In the present advanced age, information has turned into the soul of organizations. From little new businesses to global companies, associations are utilizing client information the executives and deals mechanization to drive their prosperity. This combination of innovation and information enables organizations to pursue informed choices, smooth out their activities, and convey customized client encounters. In this article, we'll investigate the meaning of client information on the board and deal with computerization, their advantages, and the difficulties they present in a consistently advancing business scene.

Grasping Client Information The executives

Client information the executives is the act of gathering, coordinating, and using information connected with clients and their cooperations with an organization. This information can incorporate an extensive variety of data, including contact subtleties, buy history, correspondence history, and, surprisingly, social information. The essential goal of client information the executives is to make a brought together perspective on every client, frequently alluded to as a 360-degree view, permitting organizations to more readily comprehend and draw in with their clients.

The administration of client information includes a few key parts:

Information Assortment: This stage includes gathering information from different sources, like web-based structures, virtual entertainment, client connections, and that's only the tip of the iceberg. Guaranteeing information exactness and relevance is significant.

Information Capacity: When gathered, the information should be put away safely. Numerous organizations use Client Relationship The board (CRM) frameworks or different data sets to deal with this data.

Information Incorporation: Information from various sources ought to be coordinated to make a comprehensive client profile. This includes settling copy sections and guaranteeing information consistency.

Information Examination: Investigating client information is crucial for acquiring bits of knowledge into client conduct, inclinations, and requirements. Progressed examination instruments are in many cases used to remove significant data from the information.

Information Security and Consistency: Safeguarding client information and guaranteeing consistency with information protection guidelines (like GDPR or CCPA) is of fundamental significance. Flopping in this space can prompt extreme legitimate and reputational results.

Deals Robotization: Upgrading Proficiency and Efficiency

Deals robotization alludes to the utilization of innovation and programming to computerize different parts of the deals cycle. It smoothes out errands and exercises connected with lead age, lead supporting, and shutting bargains. Deals robotization instruments have become irreplaceable for current outreach groups and proposition a few key advantages:

Lead The board: Mechanization can help track and oversee leads all the more really. Via robotizing lead scoring and directing, outreach groups can zero in on the most encouraging open doors.

Email Showcasing: Robotized email crusades empower customized correspondence at scale. This recoveries time as well as improves the probability of changing over leads into clients.

Deals Pipe The executives: Robotization devices give constant perceivability into the deals pipeline. This permits projects to settle on information driven choices and upgrade their systems.

Client Relationship The board: Deals mechanization frameworks are frequently incorporated with CRM arrangements, giving a concentrated center point to client information. This coordination guarantees that the outreach group has exceptional data to tailor their methodology.

Revealing and Examination: Mechanization produces significant information on deals execution. Breaking down this information can assist organizations with refining their deals systems and recognize regions for development.

The Cooperative energy of Client Information The executives and Deals Robotization

While client information the board and deals mechanization fill unmistakable needs, their incorporation is where their actual potential is understood. This is the way they complete one another:

Information Driven Deals: Client information the board gives the fundamental client experiences to deal with computerization to actually work. Computerization instruments can utilize this information to section clients, customize associations, and trigger robotized activities in light of client conduct.

Further developed Client Experience: The cooperative energy between these two capabilities empowers organizations to convey a more customized and responsive client experience. Deals mechanization apparatuses can use client information to send opportune messages or offers, improving commitment and fulfillment.

Deals Productivity: With a bound together client information the executives framework, deals mechanization instruments can get to an extensive perspective on every client. This works on the deals cycle, empowering agents to go with faster and more educated choices.

Information Upheld Navigation: The scientific capacities of client information the board give experiences that guide deals procedure. Organizations can follow which deals strategies are best and advance their methodology appropriately.

Scalability: As organizations develop, the coordination of these frameworks guarantees that the information foundation can adjust and extend. This versatility is fundamental to oblige expanding client information and deals activities.

Difficulties and Contemplations

While the combination of client information the executives and deals robotization is exceptionally worthwhile, it isn't without its difficulties. Here are a few contemplations:

Information Quality: Trash in, trash out. Guaranteeing the precision and nature of client information is foremost. Unfortunate information quality can prompt ineffectual computerization and misinformed deals endeavors.

Information Protection and Consistency: With expanded information utilization comes a more noteworthy obligation. Organizations should be tireless in agreeing with information protection guidelines, as any breaks can bring about extreme outcomes.

Incorporation Intricacy: Incorporating these frameworks can be actually intricate and requires cautious preparation and execution. Organizations might have to put resources into gifted staff or outsider answers to accomplish a consistent mix.

Cost: Carrying out and keeping up with hearty client information the executives and deals mechanization frameworks can be expensive. In any case, the excessively long advantages oftentimes offset the fundamental hypothesis.

Client Reception: Fruitful execution requires purchase from every pertinent group. Guaranteeing that outreach groups and different clients comprehend and actually utilize the frameworks is basic for understanding the full advantages.

Client information the executives and deals computerization are as of now not discretionary for organizations looking for outcome in the advanced age. These frameworks give the establishment to information driven direction, improved client encounters, and productive deals processes. The cooperative energy between these capabilities is where the genuine force of information is opened, empowering organizations to flourish in an undeniably aggressive scene.

Marketing and Customer Segmentation

In the realm of current promotion, personalization has turned into the foundation of progress. The times of one-size-fits-all promotion are a distant memory. All things considered, organizations are progressively going to client division as an essential way to deal with focus on their crowds successfully.

Client division is the act of separating an organization's client base into unmistakable gatherings in light of explicit qualities, ways of behaving, or inclinations. These gatherings, or portions, permit organizations to tailor their advertising endeavors to take care of the novel requirements and interests of each fragment, bringing about additional applicable and convincing efforts.

The worth of client division lies in its capacity to give a more profound comprehension of an organization's client base. This more profound knowledge is pivotal for advertisers to make exceptionally designated and pertinent substance, offers, and advancements. Here are a few key motivations behind why client division is fundamental in the present promoting scene:

Improved Focusing on: By separating clients into fragments, advertisers can recognize which gathering is probably going to be keen on a specific item or administration. This results in more productive utilization of showcasing assets, as organizations can zero in their endeavors on the most encouraging leads.

Improved Personalization: Personalization is a main impetus in present day showcasing. At the point when you understand where your listeners might be coming from well, you can make content that talks straightforwardly to their requirements and wants. Portioned crusades take into consideration customized information that reverberates with each gathering of clients.

Expanded Consumer loyalty: At the point when clients get customized offers and content that line up with their inclinations, they are bound to feel esteemed and comprehended. This can prompt more significant levels of consumer loyalty and dedication.

Streamlined Advertising Spend: Division empowers organizations to distribute their advertising financial plans all the more productively. Rather than spreading assets meagerly across a wide crowd, organizations can put more in the sections that are probably going to yield positive outcomes.

Better Item Advancement: Understanding the exceptional necessities of various client portions can illuminate item advancement. It permits organizations to make items that cook explicitly to the longings and prerequisites of specific gatherings.

There are multiple ways of moving toward client division, and the philosophy utilized may differ starting with one business then onto the next. The absolute most normal kinds of division include:

Segment Division: This partitions the crowd in light of attributes like age, orientation, pay, training, and conjugal status. For instance, an organization could make different promoting lobbies for youthful grown-ups, guardians, or retired folks.

Geographic Division: Area based division considers factors like locale, city size, environment, or metropolitan/provincial regions. It's especially valuable for organizations with items or administrations that have geological importance.

Psychographic Division: This approach centers around clients' way of life, interests, values, and ways of behaving. It assists advertisers with understanding what persuades their crowd and what sort of informing will impact them.

Social Division: By examining client ways of behaving, like buy history, site corporations, and commitment with advertising materials, organizations can bunch clients in light of their activities and inclinations.

Firmographic Division: B2B organizations frequently use firmographic division, which is like segment division yet applied to organizations. Qualities like industry, organization size, and income assume a huge part in this methodology.

Needs-Based Division: A few organizations make fragments in view of explicit necessities or trouble spots that their clients have. This approach plans to resolve these issues straightforwardly in showcasing efforts.

Effective client division requires gathering and examining information. In the advanced age, client information is more available than any other time in recent memory, on account of web based following, virtual entertainment, and client relationship with the executives (CRM) frameworks. Advertisers can utilize this information to make definite client profiles for each portion, illustrating their attributes, ways of behaving, and inclinations.

When these fragments are laid out, the subsequent stage is to make showcasing efforts custom fitted to each gathering. This might include creating interesting information, planning designated offers, or choosing the most proper channels for arriving at each portion.

Moreover, it's essential to take note that client division is certainly not a one-time exertion. Market elements, client inclinations, and company contributions can change. Along these lines, organizations should routinely reconsider and refine their division systems to guarantee their showcasing endeavors stay compelling.

Taking everything into account, client division is the key part of current showcasing. It permits organizations to comprehend their clients at a more profound level, empowering them to make exceptionally focused, customized showcasing efforts. This results in better consumer loyalty as well as advances advertising spend and drives higher return for capital invested. As showcasing keeps on developing in the computerized age, the force of client division will just turn out to be more articulated, and organizations that tackle its potential will acquire a critical upper hand.

Customer Service and Support

In the present exceptionally cutthroat business scene, client care and backing have arisen as the foundation of progress. As organizations endeavor to separate themselves on the lookout, they progressively perceive the essential job that outstanding client support plays in building and keeping up with client devotion.

In this period of elevated client assumptions, organizations that focus on client support and support get by as well as flourish.

The Development of Client assistance

The idea of client assistance isn't new, however its significance and how it's conveyed have advanced decisively throughout the long term.

By and large, client support was much of the time seen as a receptive capability - tending to client grumblings or issues when they emerged. Be that as it may, this approach is as of now not adequate.

In the advanced period, client support is about something beyond settling issues. It incorporates proactive endeavors to address client issues, expect their interests, and make a positive involvement with each touchpoint. This advancement is driven by a few variables, including:

Client Strengthening: Clients approach more data and decisions than any other time, and they anticipate an elevated degree of administration and responsiveness. Disappointed clients can without much of a stretch offer their encounters via web-based entertainment, making it significant for organizations to focus on consumer loyalty.

Technology: Progresses in innovation have changed the manner in which organizations associate with clients. Chatbots, computer based intelligence driven help, and information investigation empower organizations to give more customized and effective assistance.

Globalization: As organizations extend their scope globally, understanding different client needs and social subtleties becomes fundamental for compelling client care and backing.

The Effect of Extraordinary Client assistance

Extraordinary client care and support can significantly affect a business' prosperity. Here are a few key regions where it has an effect:

Client Maintenance: A reliable client is a significant resource. Excellent client assistance guarantees that clients stay with your image as well as turned into its backers, advancing your items or administrations to other people.

Brand Notoriety: Positive client care encounters make areas of strength for a standing. Cheerful clients are bound to prescribe your business to other people and compose positive audits web based, supporting your validity and dependability.

Income Development: Fulfilled clients are bound to make rehash buys and spend more on your items or administrations. A study by Harvard Business Survey found that clients who had the best previous encounters burn through 140% more contrasted with the people who had the least fortunate encounters.

Upper hand: In a serious market, outstanding client support can be a strong differentiator. It can help your business stick out and draw in new clients who are searching for a prevalent help insight.

Cost Reserve funds: While giving great client assistance might require speculation, it can likewise prompt expense reserve funds over the long haul. Fulfilled clients are more averse to raise objections and require broad critical thinking endeavors.

The Job of Innovation in Client support

Innovation has fundamentally reshaped the client support scene. Here are a few manners by which it has had an effect:

Simulated intelligence Controlled Chatbots: Chatbots are progressively being utilized to give moment reactions to normal client requests, opening up human specialists to deal with additional perplexing issues.

Information Examination: Examining client information assists organizations with grasping inclinations, distinguishing drifts, and customized administration, further developing the general client experience.

Omnichannel Banking: Innovation permits organizations to offer help through different channels, including telephone, email, talk, and online entertainment, guaranteeing that clients can connect in their favored manner.

Self-Administration

Entryways: Numerous clients lean toward settling their issues freely. Self-administration gateways give the devices and data they need, lessening the volume of help requests.

Remote Help: The ascent of remote work has likewise brought forth distant client care, permitting organizations to take advantage of a worldwide ability pool for their client care groups.

Best Practices in Client care and Backing

For organizations hoping to succeed in client care and backing, a few prescribed procedures ought to be thought of:

Enable Your Client care Group: Thoroughly prepared and engaged client care specialists can have a massive effect. Urge them to utilize their judgment and pursue choices to help the client.

Personalization: Use information and innovation to customize collaborations. Address clients by name and designer suggestions to their inclinations.

Ideal Reactions: Answer instantly to client requests. In a universe of moment satisfaction, sitting tight for a reaction can be baffling and harming to the client experience.

Criticism Circles: Energize client criticism and use it to work on your items and administrations. Tell your clients that their feedback is important.

Consistency Across Channels: Guarantee a predictable client experience across all correspondence channels. Clients ought to get a similar degree of administration whether they reach you through email, telephone, or visit.

Proactive Correspondence: Contact clients before they even acknowledge they have an issue. For instance, in the event that an item they as of late bought has a known bug, illuminate them and give an answer proactively.

Client care and backing have made considerable progress, developing from a responsive capability to a proactive and significant component of business achievement. In the present cutthroat scene, the nature of your client care can represent the moment of truth in your image.

Remarkable client care holds existing clients as well as draws in new ones, improves your image's standing, and drives income development. By embracing innovation and best practices, organizations can make a positive and enduring effect on their clients, getting their spot on the lookout.

Chapter 2
Benefits of
Effective CRM

In the present exceptionally serious business scene, Client Relationship The executives (CRM) has arisen as a basic device for organizations, everything being equal. Compelling CRM frameworks give a huge number of advantages, going from further developed consumer loyalty to expanded functional productivity and income development. In this paper, we will dive into the critical benefits of executing a proficient CRM framework.

Improved Consumer loyalty: Compelling CRM frameworks enable organizations to more readily grasp their clients' requirements, inclinations, and ways of behaving. This information permits organizations to give custom-made items and administrations, bringing about higher consumer loyalty. At the point when clients feel that a business comprehends and thinks often about their necessities, they are bound to stay steadfast and take part in long haul connections.

Further developed Correspondence: CRM frameworks unify client information, making it simpler for different offices inside an organization to access and share data. This results in more consistent correspondence and coordinated effort among deals, promoting, client care, and different groups. At the point when all workers have a 360-degree perspective on client corporations, they can answer requests all the more and convey a more firm client experience.

Compelling Promoting Efforts: A very much carried out CRM framework gives significant experiences into client conduct, permitting organizations to make profoundly designated showcasing efforts. This prompts more proficient expenditure of promoting assets and higher change rates. Organizations can customize showcasing messages, item proposals, and advancements to match individual client inclinations, expanding the possibilities of making a deal.

Smoothed out Deals Cycles: CRM programming helps outreach groups in overseeing leads, following connections, and finishing everything with all the more proficiently. It gives devices to lead scoring, opportunity following, and deals anticipating. Agents can focus on their endeavors, center around high-esteem leads, and give convenient reactions, which can altogether build their prosperity rates.

Expanded Income: CRM frameworks add to income development by assisting organizations with recognizing strategically pitching and upselling open doors. By examining client information and buy history, organizations can offer integral items or overhauls that line up with a client's requirements and interests. This lifts deals and client lifetime esteem.

Client Maintenance: Continuing to exist clients is in many cases more financially savvy than securing new ones. CRM frameworks empower organizations to screen client commitment, identify indications of disappointment, and go to proactive lengths to hold significant clients. By tending to worries and giving customized arrangements, organizations can lessen the beat and construct durable client connections.

Information Investigation and Detailing: CRM frameworks gather immense measures of information about client connections, deals patterns, and showcasing efforts. This information can be broken down to acquire significant experiences into business execution and client conduct. By utilizing detailing and examination highlights, organizations can pursue informed choices and adjust their systems to improve results.

Productive Client care: CRM frameworks smooth out client service processes by empowering specialists to rapidly get to client data. This outcomes in quicker issue goals and further developed client support. With a background marked by past collaborations readily available, support groups can address client requests all the more, improving the general client experience.

Scalability: As organizations develop, they need to deal with a bigger client base and more intricate tasks. CRM frameworks are versatile and versatile, making them ideal apparatuses for developing organizations. Whether a business adds new items, administrations, or colleagues, a vigorous CRM can develop to oblige evolving needs.

Upper hand: In the present serious market, giving extraordinary client support is a differentiator. Organizations that put resources into CRM frameworks gain an upper hand by offering more customized and proficient administrations. This can assist them with drawing in new clients and hold existing ones, prompting an expanded piece of the pie.

Risk Decrease: CRM frameworks help in risk the executives by guaranteeing that client information is put away safely and is consistent with information security guidelines. They likewise assist in following client cooperations, which can be significant in debate goals or evaluating. In instances of mistakes or false impressions, having a verifiable record of collaborations can safeguard both the client and the business.

Cost Proficiency: In spite of the fact that CRM frameworks require an underlying venture, they frequently bring about long haul cost reserve funds. Via mechanizing routine undertakings, further developing deals productivity, and lessening client stir, organizations can bring down functional expenses and accomplish a superior profit from speculation.

Taking everything into account, the advantages of successful CRM frameworks are broad and significant. They improve consumer loyalty, smooth out correspondence and tasks, support income, and give an upper hand. As organizations keep on perceiving the significance of keeping up serious areas of strength with connections, CRM frameworks will stay fundamental devices for outcome in the cutting edge commercial center. Organizations that put resources into and influence these frameworks actually are better situated to flourish in an undeniably client driven business world.

Increased Sales and Revenue

Expanding deals and income is an essential objective for organizations of all sizes and businesses. It's the soul of any association, driving development, maintainability, and productivity. In the present speedy and profoundly cutthroat business climate, accomplishing and supporting expanded deals and income is a test that requires a thoroughly examined procedure, development, and versatility.

Quite possibly the most significant consideration helping deals and income is understanding your objective market. This includes directing statistical surveying to recognize client requirements, inclinations, and trouble spots. It's tied in with understanding your clients better than they know themselves. Through top to bottom examination of segment information, client overviews, and concentrating on shopper conduct, organizations can fit their items and administrations to exactly fulfill client needs.

When you comprehend your objective market, the following stage is fostering a convincing incentive. Your incentive separates your item or administration from the opposition. It ought to obviously impart the exceptional advantages and benefits your contribution gives. Compelling marking and showcasing assume a crucial part in passing this offer on to your interest group, making serious areas of strength for an important impression.

Besides, laying out serious areas of strength for a presence is fundamental in the computerized age. This incorporates having an easy to use site, dynamic online entertainment profiles, and a vigorous internet business stage. A rising number of shoppers are going to the web to find, examine, and buy items and administrations. Subsequently, a solid web-based presence is fundamental for arriving at a more extensive client base and catching deals potential open doors.

Enhancing your deals channels is another methodology that can prompt expanded deals and income. Rather than depending entirely on an actual store, organizations can investigate different deals channels, including internet business, portable applications, outsider commercial centers, and the sky's the limit from there. This more extensive reach can assist with catching a more extensive client base and drive deals development. Also, venturing into worldwide business sectors can open up new income streams, as worldwide open doors offer critical potential for organizations to flourish.

Successful evaluating techniques can essentially affect deals and income. Cautiously deciding the right price tag for your items or administrations is fundamental. Cost excessively high, and you risk losing clients; cost excessively low, and your net revenues might endure. Utilizing dynamic valuing methodologies that adjust to advertise request and contender estimating can assist with enhancing income age.

Building solid associations with clients is a critical figure expanding deals and income. Client relationship the board (CRM) frameworks can help with keeping up with and supporting these connections. Gathering and dissecting client information permits organizations to offer customized encounters, tailor item proposals, and give excellent client support, encouraging dedication and rehash business.

In addition, unwaveringly projects and motivators can be an incredible asset to help deals. By compensating rehash clients with limits, extraordinary offers, or selective access, organizations can boost faithfulness and rehash buys. These projects increment deals as well as add to verbal exchange showcasing, drawing in new clients through suggestions from fulfilled clients.

Deals and promoting endeavors should be firmly adjusted to boost their effect. Joint effort among deals and promoting groups guarantees that the right message contacts the perfect individuals with impeccable timing.

A very much arranged promoting methodology can produce leads, and a thoroughly prepared outreach group can change over those leads into clients. Customary correspondence and information dividing among these divisions can prompt higher proficiency and deal development.

As well as zeroing in on outside factors, organizations ought to likewise improve their interior activities to drive income development. Further developing efficiency and effectiveness can prompt expense investment funds and a more lithe activity. Smoothing out processes, lessening waste, and putting resources into innovation can assist organizations with working at their maximized execution, empowering them to create more income with similar assets.

To lift deals and income, organizations ought to put resources into worker preparation and advancement. A spurred and thoroughly prepared outreach group can significantly affect marketing projections.

Consistent preparation guarantees that the salesforce remains refreshed on item information and deals procedures, which eventually prompts higher transformation rates and income development.

In the present information driven world, examination and experiences assume an urgent part in driving deals and income development.

By utilizing information and progressed investigation apparatuses, organizations can acquire significant experiences into client conduct, market patterns, and deals execution.

This information driven approach empowers organizations to pursue informed choices and improve their techniques, at last expanding deals and income.

Another procedure that can add to expanded deals and income is upselling and strategically pitching. Urge clients to buy related or integral items or administrations, in this manner expanding the typical exchange esteem. This approach creates extra income as well as improves the general client experience.

Creative advancements like computerized reasoning (artificial intelligence) and AI are turning out to be progressively significant in the mission for higher deals and income.

These innovations can mechanize errands, improve personalization, and give prescient examination to recognize potential deals and amazing open doors. By embracing artificial intelligence and AI, organizations can remain in front of the opposition and accomplish income development.

Client input is an important asset for development. By effectively looking for and standing by listening to client input, organizations can recognize regions for development and advancement.

Addressing client concerns and ideas can prompt better items, administrations, and client encounters, which, thus, can bring about expanded deals and income.

All in all, expanding deals and income is a multi-layered challenge that requests a comprehensive methodology. Organizations should comprehend their objective market, foster a convincing offer, lay out major areas of strength for a presence, differentiate deals channels, execute successful evaluating systems, fabricate solid client connections, adjust deals and promoting endeavors, improve inward tasks, put resources into worker preparing, influence information and investigation, and embrace imaginative innovations. By decisively tending to these viewpoints, organizations can open their full income potential and accomplish manageable development in a profoundly serious business scene.

Improved Customer Retention

Client maintenance is a significant part of any business' prosperity. It's generally expected to be more financially savvy to hold existing clients than to procure new ones. Subsequently, organizations are continually looking for ways of further developing client maintenance. In this article, we'll investigate different methodologies and strategies to upgrade client maintenance.

Understanding Client Needs:

The underpinning of client maintenance lies in understanding and addressing client needs. To hold clients, organizations should offer items or administrations that satisfy their prerequisites. This implies directing exhaustive statistical surveying and utilizing client criticism to make enhancements.

Personalization:

Personalization is critical to causing clients to feel esteemed and comprehended. Organizations can utilize information investigation and client relationship the board (CRM) frameworks to assemble bits of knowledge about individual client inclinations. This data can be utilized to make custom fitted encounters, item proposals, and designated promoting efforts.

Phenomenal Client assistance:

Top notch client care is a foundation of client maintenance. Clients recollect their cooperations with a business, and excellent help can have an enduring positive impression. This incorporates giving quick reactions to requests, resolving issues speedily, and guaranteeing a wonderful client experience at each touchpoint.

Faithfulness Projects:

Faithfulness programs boost rehash business. These projects can take many structures, for example, focused based frameworks, limits, or elite admittance to exceptional occasions or items. The key is to compensate and perceive steadfast clients, which urges them to make want more.

Compelling Correspondence:

Keeping clients informed about new items, administrations, or advancements is fundamental. Email promoting, virtual entertainment, and other computerized channels offer savvy ways of keeping in contact with clients. Convenient and significant correspondence can reignite interest and keep clients locked in.

Input and Improvement:

Organizations ought to effectively look for input from clients and use it to work on their contributions. Client studies, audits, and direct input give significant bits of knowledge that can prompt item upgrades and better assistance conveyance.

Quality Affirmation:

Guaranteeing steady quality in items or administrations is imperative. A decrease in quality can rapidly prompt client stir. Carrying out thorough quality control measures and constant improvement cycles can assist with keeping up with elevated expectations.

Cutthroat Estimating:

While quality is fundamental, valuing likewise assumes a critical part in client maintenance. Organizations should work out some kind of harmony between offering cutthroat costs and keeping up with productivity. Consistently surveying the evaluating procedure in contrast with contenders is fundamental.

Accommodation and Availability:

Make it as simple as feasible for clients to draw in with your business. This incorporates having an easy to understand site, a versatile application, or an actual area that is helpful to get to. Diminishing rubbing in the client venture supports maintenance.

Local area Commitment:

Building a local area around your image can cultivate client faithfulness. This can be accomplished through virtual entertainment gatherings, discussions, or occasions where clients can interface with one another and with the brand.

Worker Preparing:

Thoroughly prepared and propelled representatives are bound to give magnificent client assistance. Organizations ought to put resources into continuous preparation for their staff to guarantee they have the information and abilities to address client issues really.

Information Security and Protection:

During a time of expanding information breaks and protection concerns, clients esteem organizations that focus on the security of their own data. Guaranteeing strong information assurance measures and straightforward security arrangements can improve trust and client maintenance.

Shock and Enjoyment:

At times astonishing clients with unforeseen prizes, customized messages, or little gifts can make a positive profound association with the brand. These signals can pass on an enduring effect and urge clients to remain steadfast.

Reliable Marking:

A solid and reliable brand picture helps clients recall and relate to your business. Consistency in marking, informing, and visual personality builds up the client unwaveringly.

Observing and Measurements:

To further develop client maintenance, you should gauge it. Key execution pointers (KPIs) like client degree of consistency, stir rate, and client lifetime worth can give significant bits of knowledge into the adequacy of maintenance methodologies.

All in all, further developed client maintenance is a diverse exertion that expects organizations to figure out their clients, offer remarkable support, and consistently adjust to changing inclinations and requirements. By carrying out a blend of the procedures referenced above, organizations can improve client dependability, diminish stir, and at last accomplish supportable development. Keep in mind, holding existing clients isn't just financially savvy yet in addition a demonstration of the quality and worth of your items or administrations.

Enhanced Customer Loyalty

In the exceptionally cutthroat scene of the present business world, constructing and keeping up with client dependability is fundamental for long haul achievement. Improved client dedication isn't simply a trendy expression; it's an essential objective. Organizations that focus on client dependability can make a reliable client base that gives steady income as well as goes about as brand advocates, drawing in new clients. In this article, we will investigate the idea of improved client dedication, its significance, and techniques for accomplishing it.

Figuring out Client Dedication

Client dependability alludes to areas of strength for the or connection that clients have towards a specific brand or organization. It's a proportion of the client's tendency to pick a particular item or administration more than once over other options, regardless of whether those choices are promptly accessible or less expensive. This devotion is driven by the general experience a client has with a brand, including the nature of items or administrations, client assistance, and close to home associations.

Upgraded client steadfastness makes this idea a stride further. It implies holding clients as well as extending their association with the brand. Clients who are happy with your items or administrations as well as feel a sense of having a place or profound association are bound to become faithful supporters for your image.

The Significance of Upgraded Client Faithfulness

Consistent Income Stream: Steadfast clients give a predictable income stream. They return to your business for rehash buys, decreasing the requirement for exorbitant client obtaining endeavors.

Cost-Efficiency: It's more financially savvy to hold existing clients than to procure new ones. Upgraded client steadfastness brings down the client securing cost, saving your business important assets.

Brand Backing: Steadfast clients frequently become advocates for your image. They allude loved ones, compose positive audits, and draw in with your substance via online entertainment, adding to natural development.

Versatility in Market Variances: During monetary slumps or market changes, organizations with a solid base of steadfast clients are better prepared to endure the hardship. Faithful clients keep on supporting your business, in any event, when extra cash is diminished.

Upper hand: In exceptionally cutthroat business sectors, client dedication can be a key differentiator. A business with a standing for excellent client care areas of strength for and connections will stick out.

Procedures for Improving Client Devotion

Personalization: Use information driven bits of knowledge to customize the client experience. Figure out your clients' inclinations and conduct, and design your promoting, item proposals, and correspondences in like manner.

Excellent Client care: Put resources into extraordinary client assistance. At the point when clients have an issue or question, they ought to feel appreciated, esteemed, and speedily helped.

Unwaveringly Projects: Carry out faithfulness programs that reward clients for their recurrent business. These can incorporate limits, elite access, or focused based frameworks that lead to rewards.

Steady Quality: Guarantee that the nature of your items or administrations remains reliably high. Irregularities can dissolve trust and reliability.

Local area Building: Make a feeling of local area around your image. Draw in clients in conversations, empower client created content, and cause them to feel like a piece of a bigger, shared insight.

Request Criticism: Effectively look for criticism from your clients and use it to make upgrades. This shows clients that you esteem their perspectives and are focused on conveying what is important to them.

Close to home Association: Foster profound associations with your clients. Share your image's qualities and mission and adjust them to the upsides of your interest group.

Straightforwardness and Trust: Be straightforward and fair in your dealings with clients. Trust is a principal building block of faithfulness.

Communication: Keep the lines of correspondence open. Routinely update clients about your items, administrations, and any significant news. Powerful correspondence can assist with keeping areas of strength for a.

Shock and Joy: Periodically, shock your devoted clients with startling prizes or badges of appreciation. This can make a magnificent encounter that reinforces their dependability.

Estimating and Overseeing Client Dependability

To upgrade client dedication, you should likewise gauge it. Different key execution pointers (KPIs) can assist with evaluating client dependability. These incorporate client consistency standards, Net Advertiser Score (NPS), client lifetime worth, and consumer loyalty scores. Consistently following these measurements permits you to distinguish regions for development and change your systems likewise.

Client relationship the executives (CRM) programming can be an important device in overseeing client reliability. It helps you coordinate and dissect client information, fragment your crowd for more designated advertising, and robotize customized correspondence.

All in all, upgrading client devotion isn't simply a business procedure; it's the foundation of economical achievement. Organizations that focus on building profound, close to home associations with their clients are better prepared to flourish in a serious and consistently evolving market. By carrying out the procedures referenced above and reliably estimating and overseeing client devotion, you can make a committed client base that supports your business as well as impels it higher than ever. Keep in mind, unwaveringly isn't just about holding clients; it's tied in with making brand advocates who will support your business.

Streamlined Sales Processes

In the present quick moving and exceptionally cutthroat business climate, having a clear cut and effective deals process is fundamental for progress. Smoothed out deals processes are the establishment whereupon organizations construct their income age systems. This approach permits organizations to upgrade their deals endeavors, further develop consumer loyalty, and eventually help their primary concern.

Characterizing the Business Interaction

Prior to jumping into the advantages of smoothed out deals processes, we should characterize what a deals cycle is. A deals interaction is an organized arrangement of steps that an outreach group follows to distinguish, qualify, and close arrangements. These means might shift starting with one organization then onto the next, however they commonly incorporate prospecting, lead age, lead capability, arrangement show, exchange, and shutting.

The Significance of Smoothed out Deals Cycles

Smoothing out the deals interaction includes killing superfluous advances, robotizing monotonous errands, and guaranteeing a smooth change starting with one phase then onto the next. Here's the reason this is essential:

a. Effectiveness: A smoothed out deals process lessens the time and exertion expected to move a possibility from the underlying contact to a settled negotiation. By dispensing with excess advances, outreach groups can zero in on exercises that drive income.

b. Consistency: Normalized processes guarantee that each prospect is dealt with reliably. This consistency is imperative for keeping a positive brand picture and guaranteeing an elevated degree of consumer loyalty.

c. Information Driven Navigation: Smoothed out processes give the information expected to break down what works and what doesn't. By following each phase of the deals cycle, associations can distinguish bottlenecks and make information driven enhancements.

d. Further developed Anticipating: With a distinct deals process, it becomes more straightforward to precisely figure deals income. This is basic for planning, asset portion, and by and large business arranging.

Moves toward Smooth out Deals Cycles

Smoothing out deals processes doesn't work out by accident more or less. It requires cautious preparation, investigation, and consistent improvement. Here are a vital stages to accomplish smoothed out deals processes:

a. Map Your Current Cycle: Begin by recording your ongoing deals process. Distinguish each step and the assets expected at each stage. This will give a reasonable image of the work process.

b. Recognize Bottlenecks: Examine the current interaction to distinguish bottlenecks or regions where arrangements will generally slow down. These are regions that need consideration and improvement.

c. Computerize Dreary Errands: Use innovation to robotize monotonous and tedious errands. CRM programming, for instance, can assist with overseeing leads, track correspondences, and timetable subsequent meet-ups.

d. Normalize Correspondence: Guarantee that your outreach group follows normalized correspondence techniques. This incorporates email layouts, call contents, and show materials.

e. Give Preparing and Backing: Put resources into the preparation and improvement of your outreach group. Guarantee they have what it takes and information expected to succeed in their jobs.

f. Execute an Input Circle: Make a system for social occasion criticism from your outreach group. They are on the cutting edges and can give significant bits of knowledge into what's working and so forth.

g. Persistently Move along: Deals cycles ought not be static. Routinely audit and update your cycles in light of criticism, changing economic situations, and developing client needs.

Estimating Achievement

To decide the adequacy of your smoothed out deals processes, you want to lay out key execution markers

(KPIs) and track them over the long haul. Some fundamental KPIs include:

a. Change Rate: Measure the level of leads that move from one phase of the business interaction to the following. A higher change rate demonstrates a more smoothed out process.

b. Deals Cycle Length: Track the typical time it takes to finalize a negotiation. A more limited deals cycle is an indication of productivity.

c. Win Rate: Work out the level of arrangements that outcome in an effective deal. A higher success rate recommends that your outreach group is viable at shutting bargains.

d. Consumer loyalty: Gather criticism from clients to check their degree of fulfillment with the deals interaction. Fulfilled clients are bound to become recurrent purchasers and allude others.

e. Income Development: Eventually, income development is a pivotal measurement. A very much organized and smoothed out deals cycle ought to prompt an expansion in deals income.

Genuine Models

A few organizations have effectively carried out smoothed out deals processes and received the rewards. Salesforce, a main CRM supplier, utilizes its own innovation to smooth out its deals tasks. By incorporating CRM with different devices and mechanizing processes, Salesforce has accomplished an additional effective deals process that has added to its proceeds with development.

Another model is HubSpot, a promoting and deals programming organization. HubSpot's inbound showcasing and deals philosophy have assisted them with drawing in, draw in, and please clients with a smoothed out and client driven approach.

All in all, smoothed out deals processes are a basic part of an effective business methodology. They improve proficiency, consistency, and information driven navigation. By following an organized way to deal with smooth out deals processes, organizations can decrease costs, further develop consumer loyalty, and at last drive income development. In a quickly developing business scene, associations that focus on the improvement of their business cycles will have an upper hand and flourish over the long haul.

Chapter 3
Implementing CRM Strategies and Setting Clear Objectives

Client Relationship The executives (CRM) is an urgent part of present day business tasks. It rotates around overseeing and supporting associations with clients to guarantee long haul faithfulness and fulfillment. To really execute CRM systems, setting clear targets that guide the whole process is fundamental. In this article, we will dig into the significance of CRM, the means associated with its execution, and the meaning of setting clear goals.

The Meaning of CRM

In the present profoundly cutthroat business scene, keeping serious areas of strength for a devoted client base is more basic than any other time in recent memory. CRM helps organizations assemble and support these significant connections. It includes gathering, investigating, and using client information to tailor communications, further develop client assistance, and lift deals and consistency standards.

The advantages of executing CRM procedures are various. It, right off the bat, permits organizations to acquire a more profound comprehension of their clients. By gathering and breaking down information on client conduct and inclinations, organizations can make more customized and designated promoting efforts. This prompts higher change rates and expanded consumer loyalty.

Furthermore, CRM helps in smoothing out business processes. It wipes out redundancies and shortcomings by concentrating client information and giving simple admittance to significant offices, bringing about smoother activities. This, thus, improves client support and fulfillment as requests are tended to all the more instantly and precisely.

Thirdly, CRM techniques are significant for following client connections and criticism. This data is significant for recognizing possible issues, tending to worries, and making enhancements. The capacity to answer proactively to client input can keep little issues from growing into serious issues and upgrade brand notoriety.

Finally, CRM can support income through up-selling and strategically pitching valuable open doors. By understanding client needs and ways of behaving, organizations can suggest integral items or administrations, expanding the typical exchange esteem. Besides, it helps in holding existing clients, which is many times more financially savvy than gaining new ones.

Executing CRM Methodologies

The effective execution of CRM methodologies includes a few key stages:

Survey Present status: Prior to jumping into CRM execution, assessing the current cycles and frameworks in place is fundamental. Comprehend how client information is gathered, put away, and utilized. Recognize qualities and shortcomings to pinpoint regions for development.

Set Clear Goals: Clear goals are the underpinning of any CRM procedure. Characterize what you need to accomplish with CRM, whether it's further developing client support, expanding deals, or upgrading consumer loyalty. Goals ought to be explicit, quantifiable, reachable, significant, and time-bound (Brilliant).

Select the Right CRM Programming: Picking the fitting CRM programming is a basic choice. The product ought to line up with your targets and be not difficult to incorporate with existing frameworks. It ought to likewise offer the fundamental highlights, for example, information investigation, mechanization, and detailing apparatuses.

Information Assortment and Joining: Gather and coordinate client information from different sources, like deals, showcasing, and client assistance. This solidified information turns into the establishment for customized client collaborations.

Representative Preparation: Appropriate preparation is essential to guarantee that your workers can successfully utilize the CRM framework. They ought to know about its elements and comprehend how to utilize client information to upgrade their corporations.

Computerize Cycles: Use CRM programming to computerize routine undertakings, for example, sending follow-up messages, following client corporations, and fragmenting clients in view of their way of behaving. Computerization decreases manual work and guarantees consistency.

Investigate and Decipher Information: Routinely examine client information to distinguish patterns and examples. This data can direct navigation and help in fitting advertising methodologies to individual clients or sections.

Client Criticism and Improvement: Consistently assemble and examine client criticism. Utilize this data to make upgrades to your items, administrations, and client connections.

Cross-Useful Cooperation: Advance coordinated effort between divisions, like advertising, deals, and client support. CRM ought to be a device that improves correspondence and collaboration among these groups.

Screen and Adjust: Screen the headway of your CRM system and make important changes. In the event that targets are not being met, or on the other hand assuming client inclinations change, be prepared to in like manner alter your methodology.

Setting Clear Targets

Setting clear and obvious goals is vital to the progress of CRM techniques. Goals act as a guide that directs each part of the CRM execution process. Here are a few key contemplations while setting CRM goals:

Specificity: Goals ought to be explicit, ruling out equivocalness. Keep away from ambiguous proclamations like "further develop client care." All things considered, be exact, for example, "decrease reaction time to client requests by 20%."

Measurability: Guarantee that your goals are quantifiable. You ought to have the option to track and quantify progress. Quantifiable goals permit you to check the viability of your CRM system.

Achievability: Goals ought to be reasonable and feasible. Defining impossible objectives can prompt disappointment and demotivation. Consider the assets and abilities of your association while setting targets.

Relevance: Targets should line up with the more extensive objectives and mission of your business. They ought to add to the general achievement and development of the association.

Time-bound: Relegate a time period to every goal. Setting cutoff times makes a need to get a move on and helps in arranging and prioritization.

For example, on the off chance that an organization's goal is to "increment client degrees of consistency by 15% inside the following year," this goal is explicit, quantifiable, reachable, important, and time-bound. It gives an unmistakable course to the CRM procedure, with a quantifiable result and a timetable for accomplishing it.

All in all, CRM is an imperative part of current business tasks that can yield various advantages, including further developed client connections, smoothed out processes, and expanded income. To effectively carry out CRM systems, setting clear, distinct goals that guide the whole process is urgent.

Choosing the Right CRM Software

Client Relationship The board (CRM) programming has turned into a basic instrument for organizations, everything being equal. In a time where client centricity is critical to progress, CRM programming assists associations oversee and support associations with their clients. Be that as it may, with plenty of choices accessible on the lookout, choosing the right CRM programming can be an overwhelming undertaking. This article dives into the basic elements to consider while picking the right CRM programming, guaranteeing that your business goes with a very much educated choice.

Characterize Your Objectives and Requirements:
Prior to plunging into the ocean of CRM choices, characterizing your targets and requirements is fundamental. What is it that you need to accomplish with CRM programming? Do you want it essentially for deals, showcasing, client assistance, or the entirety of the abovementioned? Understanding your particular necessities is the groundwork of choosing the right CRM programming.

Scalability:
Your business is probably going to develop, and your CRM framework ought to have the option to develop with it. Guarantee that the CRM programming you pick is versatile and can oblige your growing client base and advancing business processes.

Usability:
An easy to understand point of interaction is indispensable for fruitful CRM reception. The CRM programming ought to be natural and simple for your group to explore. Consider a framework that offers preparing and supporting assets.

Mix Capacities:
CRM programming doesn't exist in segregation. It is necessary to incorporate consistently with your current apparatuses, like email, promoting robotization, and bookkeeping programming. Guarantee that the CRM you pick has hearty combination capacities.

Portable Availability:

In the present portable world, your group ought to have the option to get to CRM information in a hurry. Ensure the CRM programming offers a versatile application or responsive web interface for simple access from cell phones and tablets.

Customization:

Organizations have interesting work processes and cycles. Your CRM ought to be adjustable to line up with your particular requirements. Search for programming that permits you to tailor fields, structures, and work processes.

Information Security:

Client information is delicate, and it's your obligation to safeguard it. Pick a CRM that has hearty safety efforts set up, like encryption, information reinforcements, and client access controls.

Cost and return for money invested:

Think about your financial plan and the profit from speculation (return for capital invested) you anticipate from the CRM. Assess both the forthright expenses and progressing costs, including membership charges, preparing expenses, and potential customization costs.

Client assistance:

Phenomenal client care can be a lifeline when you experience issues or need help with your CRM. Actually take a look at the seller's standing for giving brief and supportive client service.

Client Input and Audits:

Understanding audits and looking for criticism from current clients of the CRM programming you're thinking about can give significant experiences into its certifiable presentation and impediments.

Industry-Explicit Highlights:
A few organizations require industry-explicit elements in their CRM. On the off chance that your industry has exceptional requirements, investigate CRM choices intended for your area.

Examination and Announcing:
Information driven navigation is pivotal in the present business climate. Guarantee the CRM programming offers vigorous investigation and revealing elements to assist you with removing important experiences from client information.

Compliance:
Contingent upon your industry and area, there might be legitimate and administrative consistency prerequisites for overseeing client information. Ensure the CRM programming lines up with these guidelines.

Preparing and Onboarding:
Carrying out another CRM can be troublesome. Check assuming the seller offers preparing and onboarding administrations to facilitate the progress for your group.

Long haul Suitability:
Think about the merchant's soundness and long haul reasonability. You would rather not put resources into a CRM programming that could vanish in a couple of years.

Free Preliminaries and Demos:
Most CRM suppliers offer free preliminaries or demos. Exploit these to get an involved encounter and assess how well the product meets your requirements.

Client Input and Audits:

Understanding audits and looking for criticism from current clients of the CRM programming you're thinking about can give important bits of knowledge into its true exhibition and impediments.

All in all, picking the right CRM programming is a crucial choice for your business. It can smooth out your activities, upgrade client connections, and lift your primary concern. By characterizing your necessities, taking into account factors like versatility, convenience, joining, customization, information security, and the sky's the limit from there, and directing careful exploration, you can pursue an educated decision that lines up with your business targets. Keep in mind, a CRM is a drawn out venture, so take as much time as is needed to track down the ideal fit for your association.

Data Collection and Analysis

In the advanced period, information has turned into the soul of associations and organizations across the globe. The determined computerized change has made ready for a phenomenal storm of information, from marketing projections and client criticism to weather conditions and virtual entertainment posts. This abundance of data can possibly open important experiences and drive informed navigation, yet just when gathered and investigated successfully. In this investigation of information assortment and examination, we will dig into the meaning of these cycles, their systems, and their applications in different spaces.

The Meaning of Information Assortment and Examination

Information assortment and examination are significant in a horde of spaces. They establish the groundwork for proof based dynamics in areas as different as business, medical care, schooling, and even arrangement making. We should separate why information is fundamental and how its assortment and examination drive progress.

1. Informed Navigation: At the center, information assortment and examination enable associations and people to settle on informed choices. By inspecting past patterns, recognizing designs, and projecting future situations, information driven choices lead to improved results.

2. Further developed Proficiency: In business, information assortment and examination can advance tasks, from store network the executives to promoting techniques. This effectiveness saves assets as well as upgrading client encounters.

3. Personalization: In the time of web based business and online administrations, information examination is instrumental in conveying customized encounters. By understanding client inclinations and conduct, organizations can fit their contributions to match individual requirements.

4. Medical services Progressions: In the field of medical services, information examination upholds illness research, therapy improvement, and early analysis. It has additionally demonstrated fundamentals during worldwide wellbeing emergencies like the Coronavirus pandemic, supporting following and understanding the infection's spread.

5. Logical Disclosures: The domain of logical examination intensely depends on information assortment and investigation. Whether it's revealing the secrets of the universe, concentrating on environmental change, or finding new medications, information fills in as the reason for weighty disclosures.

6. Metropolitan Preparation and Strategy: City organizers and policymakers use information to plan and execute programs that benefit networks. From traffic the board to general wellbeing drives, information driven choices can upgrade personal satisfaction in metropolitan conditions.

The Course of Information Assortment

Information assortment is the underlying move toward the information examination process. It includes gathering important data from different sources. The information gathered might be quantitative (mathematical) or subjective (non-mathematical), and it can emerge from essential or optional sources. We should dig into the critical parts of information assortment.

1. Information Sources: Information can be gathered from many sources, including overviews, sensors, virtual entertainment, meetings, and openly available reports. The decision of source relies upon the particular examination or investigation objectives.

2. Information Assortment Techniques: Specialists utilize various techniques to gather information, like organized surveys, perception, and exploratory investigations. The decision of strategy is affected by the idea of the information and the exploration goals.

3. Sampling: Much of the time, gathering information from a whole populace is unfeasible or excessively expensive. Examining includes choosing a subset of the populace to address the entirety. The decision of inspecting strategy and test size is significant to guarantee the information's dependability.

4. Information Approval and Quality Confirmation: Guaranteeing the exactness and unwavering quality of gathered information is principal. This includes approval processes, including checks for fulfillment, consistency, and information section blunders.

5. Moral Contemplations: Information assortment should comply with moral rules, particularly while managing touchy or individual data. Scientists should acquire educated assent and safeguard the security regarding people.

The Workmanship and Study of Information Investigation

Information investigation is the most common way of changing crude information into significant data, frequently including factual methods and programming instruments. Viable information examination can uncover patterns, connections, and experiences. We should investigate the different features of information examination.

1. Information Cleaning: Before examination can start, information frequently should be cleaned. This includes taking care of missing qualities, anomalies, and irregularities in the dataset to guarantee the information's honesty.

2. Spellbinding Investigation: Elucidating measurements, similar to mean, middle, and standard deviation, are utilized to sum up and introduce the information in a brief way. This underlying step gives an outline of the information's focal inclinations and scattering.

3. Inferential Investigation: Inferential insights are utilized to make forecasts and reach inferences about a bigger populace in light of an example. Theory testing and certainty spans are normal devices in this stage.

4. Exploratory Information Examination (EDA): EDA includes envisioning information through procedures like histograms, disperse plots, and box plots. These visuals can uncover examples and connections that probably won't be obvious from crude information.

5. Prescient Displaying: Prescient examination use calculations and AI strategies to gauge future results or patterns. This is significant in fields like money for stock cost expectations or in medical services for sickness risk appraisal.

6. Understanding and Detailing: Information examination is unfinished without the translation of discoveries. Examiners need to make an interpretation of factual outcomes into significant bits of knowledge. The last step frequently includes planning reports or introductions to convey these discoveries.

Applications in Different Fields

The force of information assortment and investigation is clearly obvious across various areas. Here are a few useful applications that feature the effect of these cycles:

1. Business and Showcasing: Retail organizations use information to improve stock administration and designer showcasing efforts. Internet business stages prescribe items to clients in light of their perusing and buy history.

2. Healthcare: Clinics and exploration organizations use information to foresee illness flare-ups, upgrade treatment designs, and recognize patient gamble factors. Wearable gadgets gather continuous wellbeing information, empowering people to screen their prosperity.

3. Education: Schools and colleges use information to survey understudy execution, recognize regions for development, and designer educational methodologies to individual learning styles.

4. Natural Science: Environment researchers examine tremendous datasets to screen changes in worldwide temperatures, ocean levels, and fossil fuel byproducts. This data is urgent for understanding and alleviating the impacts of environmental change.

5. Government and Strategy: Legislatures use information to illuminate strategy choices, allot assets, and measure the effect of projects. Evaluation information, for instance, decides political portrayal and asset conveyance.

6. Finance: Venture companies and banks depend on information investigation to oversee portfolios, anticipate market drifts, and relieve chances. Credit scoring frameworks evaluate a singular's reliability utilizing authentic monetary information.

Difficulties and Future Patterns

While information assortment and investigation offer extraordinary potential, they additionally present difficulties and moral contemplations. One huge test is the sheer volume of information created everyday. The expression "huge information" has arisen to portray datasets so gigantic that they require specific instruments and procedures for investigation. Also, protection concerns have become central, with information breaks and abuse of individual data raising alerts.

To address these difficulties, information science is developing with new advances and strategies. Man-made consciousness (computer based intelligence) and AI are being utilized to mechanize the investigation of enormous datasets, making it conceivable to precisely extricate experiences quicker and that's just the beginning. Besides, information morals and protection guidelines are being built up to guarantee the mindful utilization of information.

All in all, information assortment and examination have become crucial devices for people, organizations, and society overall. The capacity to accumulate, process, and decipher information offers uncommon open doors for informed independent direction and advancement across different spaces. With the right methods, devices, and moral contemplations, we can saddle the force of information to address complex difficulties and open additional opportunities in the years to come.

Integration with Sales and Marketing

Coordination among deals and showcasing is urgent for the progress of any business. These two offices, frequently seen as unmistakable substances, ought to work as one to drive income and encourage client connections. In this 700-word investigation, we will dig into the meaning of reconciliation among deals and promoting, its advantages, difficulties, and procedures for accomplishing a consistent joint effort.

The Meaning of Joining

The detachment among deals and promoting has been a well established hierarchical standard, however it's undeniably being tested in light of multiple factors. In the present exceptionally cutthroat business scene, clients are more educated and knowing than any time in recent memory. They expect a reliable and customized insight all through their purchasing process. To live up to these assumptions, it's pivotal for deals and advertising groups to team up and adjust their endeavors.

Client   Driven Approach: Combination among deals and promoting guarantees a brought together methodology zeroed in on the client. Outreach groups have important experiences into client necessities and inclinations, which can illuminate promoting systems. While showcasing and deals are in a state of harmony, they can fit content and missions to address the particular trouble spots and wants of likely purchasers.

Effective Lead The executives: One of the main benefits of mix is further developed lead the executives. Advertising produces leads, and deals changes over them into clients. A consistent handover of leads from showcasing to deals, with clear rules and data, smoothes out the deals interaction. It diminishes the gamble of leads escaping everyone's notice, bringing about expanded transformation rates and income.

Information   Driven Direction: Showcasing and deals produce an abundance of information. At the point when these offices cooperate, they can use information examination to acquire further experiences into client conduct and inclinations. This information driven approach helps in refining showcasing efforts and deals techniques for improved results.

Consistency in Informing: Conflicting informing can confound and estrange likely clients. At the point when deals and showcasing groups team up, they can guarantee that the messages passed on to possibilities are reliable. This consistency fabricates trust and a solid brand picture.

Advantages of Joining

The joining among deals and promoting isn't just about separating storehouses; it yields various unmistakable advantages for organizations.

Higher Income: Incorporated deals and advertising endeavors lead to expanded deals and income. The arrangement guarantees that promoting efforts reverberate with the main interest group, making it simpler for outreach groups to close arrangements.

Cost Effectiveness: Mix lessens excess endeavors and exorbitant covers in advertising and deals exercises. It helps in upgrading asset assignment and bringing down procurement costs.

Further developed Client Maintenance: A bound together methodology implies that post-deal commitment lines up with pre-deal guarantees. This consistency cultivates trust and empowers rehash business from fulfilled clients.

Smoothed out Correspondence: Clear and open

correspondence among deals and showcasing divisions is a side-effect of combination. This results in better cooperation, prompting more successful procedures and missions.

Challenges in Accomplishing Mix

While the advantages are clear, incorporating deals and showcasing can be a complicated interaction. A few difficulties should be tended to.

Social Contrasts: Deals and showcasing groups frequently have various societies, outlooks, and objectives. Spanning these holes major areas of strength are required and changing the board.

Innovation Coordination: Current showcasing depends intensely on innovation, like Client Relationship The executives (CRM) and promoting mechanization apparatuses. Incorporating these advances with deals cycles can be challenging.

Information Sharing and Protection: The sharing of client information between divisions should conform to protection guidelines. Keeping up with information security and moral practices is fundamental.

KPI Arrangement: Deals and promoting may have different Key Execution Markers (KPIs). Adjusting these measurements to reflect shared objectives can be an intricate errand.

Systems for Effective Coordination

To accomplish effective reconciliation among deals and showcasing, associations can embrace a few techniques.

Initiative and Culture: It begins at the top with initiative advancing a culture of cooperation and arrangement.

Energize normal gatherings and cross-departmental groups to work with correspondence.

Innovation Mix: Put resources into devices that work with information sharing and mechanization. CRM frameworks that span deals and promoting are significant for a consistent progression of data.

Shared Objectives and KPIs: Characterize shared goals and KPIs that the two deals and showcasing groups are responsible for. This guarantees a brought together concentration.

Ordinary Input Circles: Make instruments for criticism from deals to advertising as well as the other way around. This aids in nonstop improvement and transformation to advertise changes.

All in all, mixing among deals and showcasing is essential in the present business scene. It prompts a client driven approach, expanded productivity, higher income, and better client maintenance. While challenges exist, associations can conquer them with the right methodologies. By encouraging cooperation and arrangement, organizations can receive the various rewards that reconciliation offers in the consistently developing universe of deals and promoting.

Chapter 4
Maximizing

Sales with CRM

In the present exceptionally cutthroat business scene, expanding deals is a first concern for organizations of all sizes and enterprises. Quite possibly the best device in accomplishing this objective is Client Relationship The executives (CRM). CRM is a complex methodology that consolidates innovation, cycles, and systems to oversee and sustain client connections. When utilized really, CRM can assist organizations with helping deals, further develop consumer loyalty, and drive development. In this article, we will investigate how CRM can be utilized to augment deals.

Grasping CRM

Prior to digging into the procedures for expanding deals with CRM, it's fundamental to have an unmistakable comprehension of what CRM is. At its center, CRM is a framework that empowers organizations to oversee and examine client cooperations all through the client lifecycle. This incorporates following leads, overseeing contacts, and sustaining associations with clients. CRM frameworks give a unified stage where all client information, collaborations, and correspondence history can be put away and gotten to. This information frames the reason for informed independent direction and designated deals procedures.

Smoothing out Deals Cycles

One of the essential ways CRM amplifies deals is by smoothing out deals processes. CRM programming offers devices for overseeing leads and open doors, following deals exercises, and computerizing routine errands. This robotization diminishes the time outreach groups spend on authoritative assignments, permitting them to zero in on selling. Moreover, CRM can give bits of knowledge into the deals pipeline, assisting groups with distinguishing bottlenecks and focus on bargains. Accordingly, agents can work all the more proficiently and finish on quicker.

Lead The board

Successful leadership of the board is significant for supporting deals. CRM frameworks are furnished with lead following and scoring abilities, permitting organizations to focus on leads in view of their expected worth. By dividing leads and appointing scores, outreach groups can focus their endeavors on the most encouraging possibilities. Besides, CRM keeps leads from escaping everyone's notice via robotizing follow-up updates and giving an exhaustive perspective on each lead's set of experiences and status.

Client Information and Bits of knowledge

An abundance of client information is gathered and put away inside CRM frameworks. This information goes a long way past contact data and incorporates past communications, buy history, inclinations, and that's just the beginning. Admittance to this data enables outreach groups to customize their connections with clients. By fitting pitches and offers to individual requirements and inclinations, salespeople can essentially expand the possibilities bringing a deal to a close.

In addition, CRM examination devices empower organizations to acquire important bits of knowledge into client conduct and patterns. This information can be utilized to distinguish strategically pitching and upselling open doors, assisting with expanding income from existing clients.

Deals Determining

Precise deals estimating is a fundamental component of boosting deals. CRM frameworks give the important information and apparatuses to make solid estimates. By breaking down authentic deals information and current pipeline data, organizations can foresee future deals with more prominent accuracy. This guides the asset portion as well as considers proactive direction and acclimations to meet deals targets.

Further developed Correspondence

CRM frameworks work with better correspondence inside outreach groups and among deals and different offices. Agents can work together more actually, sharing data about leads and clients. This organized methodology guarantees that clients get a predictable and customized insight, which can be a strong deals driver.

Besides, CRM upgrades correspondence with clients. Organizations can utilize CRM to robotize correspondence, like sending customized messages and messages brilliantly. These computerized interchanges can support leads, give refreshes on items or administrations, and even request input. Powerful and opportune correspondence can altogether influence deals changes and consumer loyalty.

Designated Promoting and Missions

CRM assumes a crucial part in designated promoting and crusades. With the information gathered, organizations can fragment their client base and make exceptionally designated showcasing drives. Whether it's sending customized email crusades, running unique proposals for explicit client fragments, or fitting substance to individual inclinations, CRM assists organizations with contacting the right crowd with the right message.

Client Maintenance

Amplifying deals isn't just about procuring new clients; it's likewise about holding existing ones. CRM helps with client maintenance by empowering organizations to construct more grounded, enduring connections. By monitoring client inclinations, buy history, and input, organizations can constantly work on their items and administrations to address client issues. A fulfilled client is bound to turn into an unwavering one, bringing about recurrent business and expanded deals.

Preparing and Execution The executives

CRM frameworks can be utilized to prepare and oversee outreach groups successfully. By observing deals exercises and results, organizations can recognize regions where preparation is required. CRM can likewise help in execution assessment by giving information in individual and group deals execution. This information can be utilized to remunerate top entertainers and distinguish regions for development.

Reconciliation with Deals Investigation

To really augment deals with CRM, it's essential to incorporate the CRM framework with deals investigation apparatuses. This empowers organizations to acquire further bits of knowledge into deals execution and client conduct. Deals investigation can reveal examples, patterns, and potential open doors that probably won't be quickly clear, taking into account more educated navigation and vital preparation.

All in all, augmenting deals with CRM isn't just imaginable yet exceptionally valuable. By smoothing out deals processes, successfully overseeing leads, saddling client information and bits of knowledge, and further developing correspondence, organizations can accomplish higher deals and income. Also, CRM assists with exact deals determining, designated advertising, client maintenance, and execution of the executives. When coordinated with deals examination, CRM turns into a crucial device for organizations hoping to acquire an upper hand in the present commercial center.

Sales Forecasting and Predictive Analytics

Deals anticipating is the method involved with assessing future deals in light of authentic information, market patterns, and other important variables. Its importance couldn't possibly be more significant, as it fills in as the establishment for basic business choices in regions, for example, planning, stock administration, and advertising systems. Here are a few key justifications for why deals estimating is critical:

Asset Assignment: Precise deals figures assist organizations with dispensing assets productively. Whether it's stock, labor, or showcasing spend, knowing what's in store as far as deals considers better assets the board.

Vital Preparation: Estimates give the premise to vital preparation. Organizations can put forth attainable objectives, change their methodologies, and go with information driven choices to remain serious.

Stock Administration: A very much determined deals plan helps with keeping the perfect proportion of stock close by. This forestalls overloading or stockouts, lessening costs and expanding consumer loyalty.

Income The executives: Deals figures are fundamental for overseeing income. They assist organizations with understanding when income is probably going to come in and when costs will be brought about.

The Force of Prescient Investigation: Prescient investigation takes deals estimating to a higher level. It includes the utilization of cutting edge factual and AI models to dissect authentic information and make forecasts about future deals, client conduct, and market patterns. Here are a few different ways prescient examination improves the deals determining process:

Information driven Experiences: Prescient examination depends on a huge measure of information, permitting organizations to reveal stowed examples and experiences that probably won't be clear through customary strategies.

Further developed Precision: Prescient models can fundamentally upgrade the precision of deals gauges. They think about a great many factors, from verifiable deals information to outside factors like financial circumstances and market patterns.

Constant Changes: Prescient investigation can adjust to evolving conditions. In the event that there is an unexpected change on the lookout or client conduct, these models can rapidly change figures to mirror the new reality.

Personalization: Prescient investigation can be applied to client information to customize promoting endeavors. This prompts more successful showcasing efforts and better client commitment.

How Deals Anticipating and Prescient Examination Work:

The course of deals estimating and prescient examination includes a few key stages:

Information Assortment: The initial step is to assemble significant information. This incorporates authentic deals information, market information, and whatever other data that could affect deals.

Information Preprocessing: The gathered information should be cleaned and ready for examination. This includes dealing with missing qualities, anomalies, and changing information if fundamental.

Model Determination: Organizations pick the fitting prescient model in light of the idea of their business and the information accessible. Normal models incorporate time series investigation, relapse examination, and AI calculations.

Preparing the Model: The choice model is prepared utilizing authentic information. This interaction includes fitting the model to the information and tweaking its boundaries.

Approval and Testing: The model's exactness is surveyed by contrasting its expectations with genuine deals information. Changes are made if important.

Deployment: When the model demonstrates preciseness, making continuous predictions can be conveyed.

Persistent Checking: Prescient examination is definitely not a one-time process. Models should be persistently observed and refreshed to guarantee their precision stays high.

Influence on Organizations:

The effect of deals estimating and prescient examination on organizations is significant. These advancements offer various advantages:

Expanded Income: By upgrading asset distribution and showcasing endeavors, organizations can expand their income. Customized promoting efforts in light of prescient examination frequently lead to higher transformation rates.

Cost Decrease: Better stock administration and asset assignment can essentially decrease costs. Organizations can limit wastage and lower working costs.

Upper hand: Organizations that utilize prescient investigation gain an upper hand. They can answer rapidly to advertise changes and client inclinations, remaining in front of the opposition.

Further developed Consumer loyalty: Customized advertising and better stock administration bring about superior consumer loyalty. Blissful clients are bound to become recurrent purchasers and brand advocates.

Information Driven Independent direction: Deals anticipating and prescient examination support information driven independent direction. Organizations are done depending on hunches or instinct; they have substantial information to direct their decisions.

All in all, deals gauging and prescient examination are key apparatuses for current organizations. They empower precise deals forecasts, information driven navigation, and further developed assets for the executives. The effect of these innovations is felt across different parts of a business, from income and cost decrease to consumer loyalty and upper hand. As the business scene keeps on developing, those that embrace deals gauging and prescient examination will be better situated for progress in a dynamic and steadily evolving commercial center.

Lead Management and Conversion

Lead the executives and transformation are fundamental parts of any business' deals and advertising procedure. They incorporate the most common way of distinguishing, supporting, and eventually changing over expected clients into paying clients. In this 700-word conversation, we'll dive into the critical parts of lead the board and change, investigating the significance of these practices and giving experiences into viable procedures.

Figuring out Lead The board:

Lead the board starts with distinguishing likely clients or leads. These leads can emerge out of different sources, including site requests, web-based entertainment associations, email memberships, and career expos. When a lead is distinguished, assembling significant data about the prospect is vital. This data commonly incorporates contact subtleties, socioeconomics, and the possibility's particular advantages or needs.

The Significance of Lead Sustaining:

Supporting leads is a basic move toward the leader's interaction. Many leads are not promptly prepared to make a purchase. They might be exploring arrangements, looking at choices, or essentially not in the right temper to purchase. Viable lead support includes remaining drawn in with these leads after some time and furnishing them with important data and content that tends to their requirements and concerns.

Lead Scoring:

To focus on leads and spotlight endeavors on those probably going to change over, lead scoring is frequently utilized. This interaction doles out a mathematical worth to each toxic on different standards, for example, their degree of commitment, the data they've given, and their fit with the organization's ideal client profile. Leads with higher scores are viewed as more "deals prepared" and get more consideration.

The Job of CRM Frameworks:

Client Relationship The executives (CRM) frameworks assume an essential part in leading the board. They help organizations sort out and follow leads, computerized processes, and guarantee that leads get opportune subsequent meet-ups. CRM frameworks additionally empower groups to team up on lead sustaining and share significant data about possibilities, working on generally speaking proficiency.

Successful Lead Change Procedures:

Eventually, the objective of the board is to change over leads into paying clients. Here are a few powerful methodologies to improve the lead change process:

Personalization: Tailor your correspondence to each toxic on their particular advantages and needs. Customized messages and offers are bound to reverberate with likely clients.

Ideal Development: Answer leads expeditiously and keep up with reliable correspondence. A postpone in answering a lead can bring about botched open doors.

Instructive Substance: Furnish leads with instructive and pertinent substance that assists them with settling on informed choices. This positions your business as an industry authority and constructs trust.

Clear Source of inspiration (CTA): Guarantee that your leads know the following stage they ought to take. A distinct CTA can direct leads toward making a buy or mentioning more data.

A/B Testing: Explore different avenues regarding various ways to deal with and recognize what turns out best for your ideal interest group. A/B testing can assist with refining your change techniques.

Client Tributes and Contextual investigations: Sharing examples of overcoming adversity and tributes from fulfilled clients can be powerful in persuading prompts to convert.

Offer Motivators: Think about offering unique advancements, limits, or elite arrangements to boost prompts make a move.

Estimating and Dissecting Results:
To further develop, lead the executives and change endeavors, it's crucial for track and break down results. Key execution pointers (KPIs, for example, transformation rates, prompt client proportions, and the time it takes to change over leads can give significant bits of knowledge. By routinely exploring these measurements, organizations can pursue information driven choices to improve their systems.

Difficulties and Arrangements:
Lead the executives and transformation are not without challenges. A few leads might be lethargic, and others might

require critical work to change over. Be that as it may, by tending to these difficulties innovatively, organizations can make progress. Relentless development, designated promoting efforts, and a profound comprehension of client trouble spots can assist with beating these deterrents.

All in all, lead the board and change are principal to a business' prosperity. Successful lead the executives guarantees that organizations distinguish, support, and focus on likely clients, while change procedures assist with transforming those leads into steadfast, paying clients. By utilizing CRM frameworks, personalization, convenient development, and information driven independent direction, organizations can streamline these cycles and drive development. Recollect that the way to effectively lead the board and transformation is a client driven approach, zeroing in on building connections and offering some incentive constantly.

Personalization and Customer Engagement

Personalization is a technique that spins around making remarkable and pertinent encounters for every client. It goes past basically knowing a client's name; it includes figuring out their inclinations, ways of behaving, and expecting their necessities. This could appear in different ways, from fitted item proposals on web based business destinations to customized email promoting efforts and, surprisingly, one-on-one client care. The pitch of personalization is to cause clients to feel esteemed and comprehended, changing them from aloof purchasers into connected and faithful brand advocates.

The groundwork of personalization lies in information. Organizations accumulate, dissect, and influence information to make a complete perspective on their clients. This information can be segment, conduct, or conditional, and it helps assemble client profiles that can be utilized to convey customized encounters. For example, Amazon utilizes a client's perusing history, buy examples, and, surprisingly, the items they've evaluated to propose important items. This individual touch improves the probability of a deal as well as makes clients want more.

Client Commitment: The Sacred goal of Business Achievement

Client commitment is the close to home association between a client and a brand. Connected with clients are not just aloof buyers; they effectively cooperate with the brand, advocate for it, and, all the more significantly, stay steadfast over the long haul. Drawing in clients is definitely not an oddball task yet a continuous cycle that spotlights on building connections, encouraging trust, and enhancing the client's insight.

Commitment can appear in changed structures - from web-based entertainment communications and email reactions to leaving item audits or prescribing the brand to loved ones. The profundity of commitment fluctuates from one client to another, yet a definitive objective is to make a local area of steadfast brand devotees who purchase your items as well as turned into your best advertisers.

The Cooperative Relationship

The connection among personalization and client commitment is cooperative. Personalization is the motor that drives commitment, and commitment, thus, energizes personalization. How about we analyze this cooperative energy:

Improved Client Experience: Personalization improves the client experience by giving custom fitted substance and proposals. At the point when clients feel comprehended, they are bound to draw in with the brand. For example, streaming stages like Netflix use personalization to suggest shows and films in light of a client's watching history, prompting expanded commitment as clients find new happy they love.

Expanded Client Devotion: As clients connect more with a brand, they become more steadfast. Faithful clients are bound to make rehash buys, yet they additionally become advocates who got the message out. By fitting connections and contributions, organizations can cultivate this devotion.

More extravagant Information for Better Personalization: Commitment creates more information. Client communications, criticism, and inclinations are important bits of knowledge that organizations can use to refine their personalization procedures. The more drawn in clients are, the more information they give, empowering organizations to ceaselessly further develop the personalization experience.

Criticism Circle: Commitment gives an input circle that permits organizations to calibrate their personalization endeavors. On the off chance that clients are not drawing in or on the other hand in the event that they give pessimistic criticism, it very well may be an indication that personalization needs change. Alternatively, positive commitment flags that personalization is in good shape.

Challenges and Moral Contemplations

While personalization and client commitment offer enormous advantages, they likewise accompany difficulties and moral contemplations. Protection concerns, information security, and the gamble of making channel bubbles are a portion of the issues that organizations should address. It's fundamental to figure out some kind of harmony among personalization and client assent, guaranteeing that clients have command over their information and the substance they get.

All in all, personalization and client commitment are the unique team that can impel organizations to outcome in the cutting edge commercial center. The cooperative connection between the two upgrades client encounters, encourages steadfastness, and gives an abundance of information to nonstop improvement. Notwithstanding, organizations should explore moral contemplations to guarantee that personalization is a shared benefit for the two brands and clients. When executed really, personalization and client commitment make a flourishing biological system where clients purchase items as well as become backers and bosses of the brands they love

Cross-Selling and Upselling

In the present serious business scene, organizations are continually looking for ways of expanding their income and benefit. Strategically pitching and upselling are two vital procedures that have acquired noticeable quality in accomplishing these goals.

Both of these techniques include offering extra items or administrations to existing clients, however they vary in their methodology and reason. This article digs into the complexities of strategically pitching and upselling, looking at their significance, methodologies, and true models.

Figuring out Strategically pitching

Strategically pitching is the act of offering related or corresponding items or administrations to a generally made client. The point is to improve the client's general insight by giving them extra arrangements that can address their issues or wants.

Strategically pitching is tied in with growing the client's bin, expanding the typical exchange worth, and making the most out of a current relationship.

One exemplary illustration of strategically pitching is the inexpensive food industry. At the point when you request a burger, the clerk frequently inquires as to whether you might want to add fries and a beverage to your request. In this situation, the burger is the essential item, and the chips and drink are correlative things. This fulfills the client's yearning as well as builds the absolute deal for the business.

Methodologies for Compelling Strategically pitching Item Arrangement: To find success at strategically pitching, the extra items or administrations offered should line up with the client's unique buy. It's critical to comprehend the client's requirements and inclinations and present choices that truly improve their experience.

Timing: The planning of the strategically pitch offer is vital. It ought to be made at a moment that the client is generally responsive and locked in. For example, in online business, a client who has quite recently added a thing to their truck might be available to ideas for related items.

Personalization: Using client information and buy history can assist with fitting strategically pitch offers. The more customized the proposal, the more probable the client is to make an extra buy.

Offer: Obviously impart the worth and advantages of the strategically pitched thing. Clients need to comprehend the reason why the extra item or administration is a significant expansion to their unique buy.

The Force of Upselling

Upselling, then again, is the act of empowering clients to overhaul or buy a more costly rendition of the item or administration they are thinking about. The essential objective of upselling is to expand the exchange esteem by persuading the client to spend more.

While this could appear to be illogical, a first rate upsell can be a shared benefit for both the client and the business.

We should consider a situation including a cell phone buy. A client may at first be keen on a mid-range cell phone, however the salesman, through powerful suggestions, persuades them to consider a better quality model with better elements. On the off chance that the client concurs, the organization expands its income, and the client leaves with a further developed item that better suits their necessities.

Procedures for Powerful Upselling

Item Information: Agents should have top to bottom information on the items and administrations they are selling. This empowers them to make sense of the advantages of a redesigned or more costly choice unhesitatingly.

Client Needs Appraisal: To upsell successfully, understanding the client's particular necessities and preferences is significant. This takes into account custom-made proposals that really benefit the client.

Make Worth: Feature the extra worth and advantages of the more costly choice. Make sense of how it can all the more likely satisfy the client's prerequisites or give an upgraded insight.

Incentives: Offer impetuses like limits or packaged arrangements to improve the upsell offer. This can make the client more leaned to overhaul.

Genuine Models

Amazon: The online business monster is prestigious for its viable strategically pitching and upselling techniques. At the point when you view an item on

Amazon, you're given a segment that recommends "Often Purchased Together" things, empowering strategic pitching. Also, Amazon frequently features better quality adaptations of items, representing upselling.

McDonald's: The cheap food goliath strategically pitches by offering feast bargains that incorporate a burger, fries, and a beverage. Clients can pick various sizes for everything, exhibiting upselling also. This basic strategy essentially expands the typical exchange esteem.

Netflix: In the domain of computerized administrations, Netflix is a perfect representation of upselling. They offer numerous membership levels, empowering clients to redesign for extra highlights like 4K streaming or more concurrent screens.

Strategically pitching and upselling are irreplaceable devices in the arms stockpile of organizations looking to expand income and upgrade consumer loyalty.

When executed in a calculated manner and morally, these practices can drive critical development while at the same time helping the client by giving custom-made arrangements and worth added choices. Organizations that put resources into grasping their clients and applying these strategies actually are bound to flourish in an undeniably serious market.

Chapter 5
Challenges and Pitfalls

Life is an excursion loaded up with various difficulties and traps. These impediments can come in different structures, from individual battles to outside factors that influence our ways. While confronting difficulties and entanglements can be overwhelming, they likewise present open doors for development and learning. In this conversation, we will investigate a few normal difficulties and entanglements that individuals experience throughout everyday life and how they can be explored.

1. Individual Difficulties:

One of the most well-known kinds of difficulties in life are the individual ones. These may incorporate medical problems, monetary battles, relationship issues, or individual uncertainties. Individual difficulties can be especially challenging to defeat since they frequently feel overpowering and segregating.

For example, an individual managing a constant sickness might confront physical and profound obstacles. It very well may be difficult to keep an uplifting perspective when confronted with continuous agony and vulnerability. In any case, numerous people who go up against such private difficulties track down versatility and strength inside themselves. They might associate with encouraging groups of people, look for clinical treatment, or utilize survival techniques to deal with their condition.

2. Profession and Instructive Difficulties:

Profession and instructive difficulties are another normal class. Numerous people experience troubles in their expert and scholarly pursuits. These can incorporate employment cutback, stagnation in a vocation, or scholastic difficulties.

Consider somebody who loses their employment because of monetary slumps. It very well may be an overwhelming disaster for their feeling of security and self-esteem. Notwithstanding, this challenge could likewise lead them to investigate new vocation potential, open doors, gain new abilities, or even go into business. Frequently, misfortunes in this space can eventually become venturing stones to better progress.

3. Relationship Difficulties:

Relationship challenges are common in everybody's life. Whether it's managing clashes with an accomplice, exploring a troublesome relational intricacy, or adapting to the furthest limit of a kinship, connections can be a wellspring of monstrous happiness and significant difficulties.

At the point when a heartfelt connection faces strife, it can prompt profound close to home torment and vulnerability about what's in store. However, many couples who conquer these difficulties arise with more grounded, stronger connections. Transparent correspondence, treatment, and self-awareness frequently assume a critical part in exploring these traps.

4. Outer Difficulties:

Outside challenges are those that emerge from factors outside of one's reach. This could incorporate catastrophic events, financial emergencies, or political flimsiness. These difficulties frequently leave individuals feeling defenseless and overpowered.

Catastrophic events, like tropical storms or tremors, can prompt far reaching obliteration and misfortune. People and networks impacted by these occasions should unite as one, look for help from government offices or NGOs, and remake their lives. Conquering outside difficulties like these frequently requires aggregate exertion and versatility.

5. Personal Difficulties:

Personal difficulties, like uneasiness, gloom, and stress, are normal and can influence individuals' regular routines. These conflicts under the surface can be similarly all around as considerable as outer impediments.

Managing psychological wellness issues can be an overwhelming excursion, yet one is best embraced with proficient assistance and backing from friends and family. Through treatment, prescription, and taking care of oneself, people can frequently track down ways of overseeing and even defeat inner difficulties.

6. Pitfalls:

Entanglements are like snares or missteps that individuals might experience in their life processes. They are frequently avoidable however now and again challenging to see until you've fallen into them.

Tarrying is a typical trap. Numerous people wind up postponing significant errands until they become earnest, causing pressure and sub-par results. Perceiving this propensity and creating time usage abilities can help forestall falling into the stalling entanglement.

Another normal trap is carelessness. It's not difficult to become OK with the norm and oppose change, in any event, when change might be fundamental for self-improvement or professional success. Keeping away from smugness includes an eagerness to get out of one's usual range of familiarity and seek after new open doors.

7. Exploring Difficulties and Entanglements:

While difficulties and entanglements can appear to be overwhelming, they are additionally valuable open doors for development and self-revelation. Here are a few techniques to successfully explore them:

Mindset: Developing a development mentality, which centers around learning and strength, can assist people with moving toward difficulties with a more inspirational perspective.

Emotionally supportive networks: Look for help from companions, family, coaches, or experts while confronting difficulties. Interfacing with others can give important bits of knowledge and consistent encouragement.

Problem-Solving: Foster critical thinking abilities to address difficulties deliberately and recognize expected arrangements.

Self-Care: Focus on taking care of oneself to keep up with physical and mental prosperity, which can assist you with better adapting to life's difficulties.

Adaptability: Embrace change and adjust to advancing conditions, as this can frequently prompt new open doors.

Gain from Slip-ups: View traps as any open doors to learn and move along. Breaking down your mix-ups can assist you with staying away from comparative traps from here on out.

All in all, difficulties and entanglements are an intrinsic piece of life. They can be private, proficient, or close to home in nature, and they frequently test our versatility and assurance. Nonetheless, with the right outlook and emotionally supportive networks, these obstructions can be changed into open doors for development and self-revelation. Exploring life's difficulties and traps is an excursion that, while testing, can at last prompt a stronger, shrewd, and satisfied life.

Data Security and Privacy Concerns

In the computerized age, information has turned into a basic resource, driving development, effectiveness, and financial development. In any case, this blast of information has additionally brought about huge worries in regards to information security and protection. As people, associations, and states depend more on computerized frameworks and the web, the dangers related with information breaks, cyberattacks, and protection infringement have heightened. This article investigates the developing scene of information security and protection concerns, featuring the difficulties and arrangements in an undeniably interconnected world.

The Information Storm and Its Difficulties

The remarkable development of information is a principal trait within recent memory. With the appearance of the web, distributed computing, and the Web of Things (IoT), we presently produce and consume tremendous measures of information everyday. This sheer volume of data presents a few difficulties concerning security and protection.

Cyberattacks: Vindictive entertainers consider this information to be a practical objective for robbery or control. Cyberattacks, for example, ransomware and phishing, have become more modern and predominant. Cybercriminals are spurred by different elements, including monetary profit, political thought processes, and even surveillance. These assaults can upset organizations, take delicate data, and compromise the security of people.

Information Breaks: Indeed, even benevolent associations are not insusceptible to information breaks. Information breaks can happen because of human mistakes, programming weaknesses, or insider dangers. When delicate data is uncovered, it can prompt wholesale fraud, monetary misrepresentation, and reputational harm for the two people and associations.

Protection Concerns: As associations gather and investigate tremendous measures of information, the line among individual and confidential data turns out to be progressively obscured. Web-based entertainment stages, web crawlers, and online retailers frequently accumulate information about people's web-based conduct and inclinations. This broad information assortment can prompt protection concerns and the gamble of individual data being abused or shared without assent.

Authoritative and Administrative Difficulties: Legislatures overall are wrestling with the need to adjust information security and protection with individual privileges and financial matters. Creating and upholding successful information insurance guidelines is an intricate errand, with fluctuating methodologies and levels of rigidity across nations.

Answers for Information Security and Protection

Because of these difficulties, there has been a developing spotlight on information security and protection arrangements. Here are a portion of the systems and innovations that mean to address these worries:

Encryption: Encryption is a crucial instrument for safeguarding information. It guarantees that regardless of whether information is captured, it stays confused to unapproved clients. Start to finish encryption, which is turning out to be progressively normal in informing applications, gives an elevated degree of protection.

Multifaceted Confirmation (MFA): MFA adds an additional layer of safety by expecting clients to give numerous types of distinguishing proof prior to accessing delicate frameworks or information. This forestalls unapproved access on the off chance that passwords are compromised.

Network protection Preparing and Mindfulness: Human blunder is a critical supporter of information breaks. Giving preparation and bringing issues to light about network safety best practices can help representatives and people perceive and stay away from normal traps.

Information Security Guidelines: State run administrations all over the planet have established information security guidelines, like the European Association's Overall Information Insurance Guideline (GDPR) and the California Shopper Protection Act (CCPA). These guidelines expect associations to be straightforward about information assortment and give people more command over their information.

Blockchain Innovation: Blockchain offers a decentralized and secure method for putting away and share information. It is known for its changelessness, making it a promising answer for getting touchy data.

Man-made reasoning (artificial intelligence) and AI: Computer based intelligence and AI can be utilized to productively identify and answer network safety dangers more. These advances can examine immense measures of information progressively to distinguish examples and inconsistencies characteristic of a break.

Adjusting Advancement and Security

While the dangers related with information security and protection are genuine and should be tended to, it's likewise crucial for figuring out some kind of harmony between safety efforts and the requirement for advancement and information driven independent direction. Inordinate safety efforts can smother progress and cut off the capability of information for positive change.

In addition, the moral ramifications of information utilization should be thought of. As associations gather and dissect information, they ought to do so dependably and morally, regarding individual privileges and protection.

All in all, information security and protection concerns are vital in the computerized age. The information storm presents critical difficulties, however there are various arrangements accessible. It's urgent for people, associations, and legislatures to cooperate to protect information while likewise regarding individual privileges and encouraging advancement. The fate of information security and protection relies upon finding some kind of harmony in an undeniably interconnected world.

User Adoption and Training,Integration Challenges

Client Reception and Preparing are significant parts of fruitful innovation executions, and they frequently remain inseparable with Incorporation Difficulties. In this article, we will investigate the significance of client reception and preparing, as well as the joining difficulties that associations face while executing new advancements.

Client Reception:
Client reception alludes to the most common way of getting end-clients to acknowledge and successfully utilize another innovation or framework inside an association. It's a basic part of any innovation execution since even the most developed and very much planned frameworks won't convey their maximum capacity on the off chance that clients don't embrace and use them really.

Protection from Change:
One of the essential provokes in client reception is protection from change. Individuals will generally be OK with their current apparatuses and processes, and the presentation of something new can be met with distrust and hesitance. This opposition can be because of dread of the obscure, worries about professional stability, or basically the inactivity of existing propensities.

To address this test, associations need to impart the advantages of the new innovation, offer clear purposes behind the change, and include workers in the dynamic cycle whenever the situation allows. Change the executives techniques and clear correspondence are fundamental in overseeing opposition.

Absence of Understanding:
Client reception is ruined when clients don't have the foggiest idea about how the new innovation functions or how it can help them in their day to day errands. This absence of understanding can prompt dissatisfaction and eventually deserting of the new framework.

Far reaching preparing programs are fundamental for span this information hole. Clients ought to be given preparation materials, studios, and progressing backing to guarantee they are sure about utilizing the innovation actually.

Inadequate Preparation:

Powerful preparation is a foundation of effective client reception. In the case of preparing is hurried, deficient, or not customized to the particular requirements of the clients, it can bring about disarray and dissatisfaction. Clients should have the option to apply what they've figured out how to their real work.

Associations ought to put resources into preparing assets, including all around organized preparing modules, proficient coaches, and valuable open doors for involved practice. The preparation ought to be progressing, as clients might need extra help as they experience certifiable situations.

Input and Client Association:

Clients frequently have significant bits of knowledge and input with respect to the innovation they are supposed to utilize. Including them in the dynamic cycle and looking for their criticism can be useful. Their feedback can assist with recognizing likely issues and open doors for development, making the innovation more easy to understand.

Incorporation Difficulties:

Joining difficulties allude to the hardships associations face while coordinating new advances into their current frameworks and cycles. These difficulties can be specialized, functional, or social and can fundamentally influence the progress of the execution.

Specialized Similarity:

One of the most well-known incorporation challenges is specialized similarity. New advances may not consistently incorporate with existing frameworks, prompting information storehouses, failures, and blunders. This issue is especially predominant in associations with heritage frameworks.

To address specialized similarity issues, associations might have to put resources into middleware or altered arrangements that work with correspondence between various frameworks. This can be a mind boggling and exorbitant cycle however is much of the time important for fruitful reconciliation.

Information Movement:

While executing new innovations, associations frequently need to move information from old frameworks to the new ones. Information relocation can be an overwhelming errand, as it includes moving enormous volumes of information while guaranteeing information uprightness and exactness.

Information movement difficulties can be moderated through cautious preparation, information purifying, and thorough testing. It's fundamental to have a vigorous information relocation procedure set up prior to leaving on the execution cycle.

Protection from Cycle Changes:

Coordination frequently includes changes to existing business processes. Representatives might be impervious to these changes, expecting that they will upset their work processes or professional stability. This obstruction can prompt deferrals and failures in the coordination cycle.

To address this test, associations ought to include workers simultaneously and obviously convey the advantages of the changes. It's essential to show how the mix will further develop effectiveness and smooth out tasks, prompting improved results for the association overall.

Security and Consistency:

With the rising spotlight on information security and consistency, incorporating new advances can present huge difficulties. Guaranteeing that information stays secure and consistent with important guidelines is a first concern for associations.

To address security and consistency challenges, associations need to lead exhaustive gamble appraisals and execute the important safety efforts. This might incorporate encryption, access controls, and consistency examining devices.

Change The board:

Changing the board is a basic part of tending to incorporation challenges. Similarly as with client reception, protection from change can prevent the combination of new advances. Clear correspondence, preparing, and commitment with workers are fundamental for overseeing change really.

All in all, client reception and preparing, alongside reconciliation challenges, are fundamental to the outcome of innovation executions. Associations should perceive the significance of resolving these issues and put resources into systems that advance client acknowledgment and consistent reconciliation. Thusly, they can augment the advantages of new advancements and accomplish their functional and vital goals.

Monitoring and Continuous Improvemen

The Substance of Checking

Checking is the course of efficiently noticing and assessing a specific part of a framework or cycle after some time. It can apply to different areas, from business tasks to self-improvement. The basic role of checking is to acquire bits of knowledge into the exhibition, recognize deviations from the ideal state, and comprehend the main drivers of such deviations. By reliably checking key execution pointers (KPIs), associations can survey their headway and pursue information driven choices.

In the business world, observing is vital. It permits organizations to watch out for their monetary wellbeing, consumer loyalty, worker execution, and that's only the tip of the iceberg. For example, marketing projections, client criticism, and creation proficiency can be ceaselessly observed. At the point when deviations happen, organizations can research the purposes for them and make restorative moves. This proactive methodology can assist with keeping minor issues from developing into serious issues.

The Force of Nonstop Improvement

Nonstop improvement is the regular development of checking. Whenever information is gathered and deviations are recognized, the following stage is to sanction changes to correct and improve what is happening. Consistent improvement is an organized way to deal with upgrading cycles, items, or administrations by making gradual changes after some time. It's frequently connected with ideas like Absolute Quality Administration (TQM), Lean Six Sigma, and Kaizen.

The way of thinking behind ceaseless improvement is that little, consistent, and progressing changes are more viable and economical than extremist changes. It cultivates a culture of learning and versatility, which can be an upper hand in a unique business scene. By utilizing information from checking, associations can go with informed choices to refine their tasks, lessen squander, increment effectiveness, and upgrade the nature of their contributions.

The Interchange of Checking and Nonstop Improvement

The connection among observing and constant improvement is harmonious. Observing gives the essential information and experiences that drive constant improvement endeavors. Without observing, associations would come up short on primary data expected to recognize regions for improvement. Consistent improvement, then again, changes the experiences acquired from observing into useful activities. These activities, thus, influence the result, which should then be observed to survey the adequacy of the changes.

This iterative cycle shapes the foundation of a well-working input circle. Take, for instance, a client care group. By checking measurements, for example, reaction time, consumer loyalty scores, and issue goal rates, the group can recognize regions that require improvement. Maybe reaction times are reliably sluggish. The group can then carry out changes, for example, extra preparation or better programming apparatuses, to resolve the issue. Checking similar measurements post-execution will uncover whether the progressions have had a positive effect or on the other hand in the event that further changes are required.

The Advantages of Observing and Constant Improvement

Both observing and constant improvement have plenty of benefits for organizations and people. For associations, these practices bring about improved effectiveness, cost investment funds, and expanded consumer loyalty. They likewise advance development and cultivate a culture of responsibility, where workers are urged to take responsibility for execution and add to the association's development.

People can likewise profit from these practices in their own and proficient lives. By laying out objectives, checking progress, and ceaselessly looking for ways of improving, people can accomplish more significant levels of efficiency, accomplish their aspirations, and become stronger notwithstanding challenges.

All in all, checking and constant improvement are basic to making progress in a consistently advancing world. The cooperative energy between these two practices permits associations and people to adjust to change, remain cutthroat, and reliably take a stab at greatness. By developing a culture of information driven independent direction and the quest for constant upgrade, organizations and people can stay at the very front of their particular fields, receiving the benefits of progressing achievement.

Chapter 6 Case Studies:Real-World Examples

Amazon: Amazon is a great representation of an organization that has become the best at CRM. They utilize a customized suggestion motor in view of client conduct and buy history. By breaking down client information, they give item suggestions, bringing about expanded deals and client maintenance.

Salesforce: Salesforce, a main CRM programming supplier, utilizes its own items widely to oversee and support client connections. By using their CRM devices, they have accomplished a noteworthy expansion in lead change and further developed client care.

Zappos: The internet based shoe and dress retailer Zappos is famous for its uncommon client care. They utilize a CRM framework that permits client care delegates to get to client information, including buy history, inclinations, and past collaborations, bringing about exceptionally customized administration.

Walmart: Walmart utilizes CRM to assemble and examine client information from different channels, remembering store buys and online associations. This information is utilized to enhance stock administration and promoting efforts, prompting better client encounters and expanded deals.

Delta Aircrafts: Delta Carriers executed a CRM framework to further develop its client support. They can follow client connections and inclinations, assisting them with giving customized encounters and addressing clients all the more productively.

Starbucks: Starbucks has a devotion program incorporated with its CRM framework. This program rewards clients for their buys and utilizes the information gathered to give customized limits and suggestions. This has prompted expanded client dedication and higher deals.

Netflix: Netflix utilizes CRM to investigate watcher information and give customized content suggestions. They utilize this data to make custom playlists for clients, bringing about longer review times and expanded supporter maintenance.

HubSpot: HubSpot, a promoting robotization and CRM stage, utilizes its own product to draw in, connect with, and charm clients. By utilizing CRM to oversee client connections and track lead data, they have developed their client base fundamentally.

Ford: Passage uses CRM to assemble information on vehicle proprietors and their administration needs. This empowers them to send customized administration updates and offers, further developing client maintenance and after-deals administration fulfillment.

Hilton Inns: Hilton utilizes CRM to deal with its visitor faithfulness program. By following client inclinations and ways of behaving, they give fitted encounters and offers to devout individuals, bringing about expanded appointments and client steadfastness.

Bayer: The drug goliath Bayer utilizes CRM to oversee collaborations with medical care experts and track deals. This has further developed correspondence and deals proficiency in the exceptionally controlled drug industry.

General Electric: GE utilizes CRM to follow its B2B client connections and oversee prospective customers. This has permitted them to smooth out their business interaction and proposition tweaked answers for their clients.

Airbnb: Airbnb utilizes CRM to oversee host and visitor collaborations. They utilize the information gathered to customize the client experience and guarantee smooth exchanges, building trust among their clients.

Walt Disney Stops and Resorts: Disney's amusement parks use CRM to further develop guest encounters. They gather information on guest inclinations and ways of behaving, permitting them to give customized proposals, plan limits, and upgrade the general guest experience.

American Red Cross: The American Red Cross uses CRM to oversee giver connections. By following giver history and inclinations, they can really draw in with benefactors, bringing about expanded commitments and progressing support.

For these situation studies, CRM framework play had a crucial impact in upgrading client connections, expanding deals, and further developing by and large business effectiveness. These models delineate the different uses of CRM across different ventures and feature the groundbreaking force of client information when utilized actually. As organizations keep on focusing on client driven approaches, CRM will stay a basic device for outcome in the cutting edge business scene.

Company A: Transforming Sales with CRM

In the present exceptionally cutthroat business scene, viable client relationships the executives (CRM) have turned into a vital device for organizations to encourage durable associations with their clients, smooth out deals processes, and at last lift income. Organization A, a groundbreaking association in the innovation area, is a perfect representation of how the essential execution of CRM can change deals tasks and drive achievement. With a client driven approach and a powerful CRM framework set up, Organization A has encountered momentous enhancements in deals execution and consumer loyalty.

Understanding Organization An's Experience

Organization A will be a moderate sized innovation firm gaining practical experience in programming improvement and IT arrangements. With a different scope of items and administrations taking special care of different businesses, keeping up with and developing its client base has forever been a first concern. In any case, in the same way as other organizations in its area, Organization A confronted difficulties in overseeing client connections effectively and boosting the capability of its deals force.

In the mission for an answer for these difficulties, Organization A perceived the groundbreaking capability of CRM innovation. CRM isn't just about overseeing client information; an essential methodology assists organizations with acquiring experiences, computerized processes, and enable their outreach groups to convey customized administration. This acknowledgment drove Organization A to leave on an excursion to upset its deals tasks.

Executing CRM: An Essential Shift

The most important phase in Organization A's CRM venture was choosing the right CRM stage. After broad exploration and interview, they picked a cloud-based CRM arrangement that offered versatility, customization, and strong investigation. This decision was imperative, as it would act as the foundation of their deals change.

With the CRM framework set up, Organization A started a complete preparation program for its outreach group. The significance of figuring out CRM's abilities, for example, lead the executives, deals anticipating, and client division, was underlined. Workers were prepared not simply on the specialized parts of the CRM yet in addition on the way of thinking behind it: putting the client at the focal point of each and every connection.

The Client Driven Approach

One of the key changes achieved by CRM at Organization A was its shift towards a client driven approach. The CRM framework gave a 360-degree perspective on every client's set of experiences, inclinations, and trouble spots. This permitted the outreach group to customize their corporations, fitting their item or administration contributions to meet every client's extraordinary necessities.

Besides, the CRM framework empowered Organization A to robotize routine undertakings, like information passage and subsequent meet-ups, permitting the outreach group to zero in more on building connections and shutting bargains. This recently discovered proficiency essentially worked in the group's efficiency, coming about in speedier reaction times and more limited deals cycles.

Information Driven Navigation

CRM isn't just about overseeing client associations yet additionally about utilizing information to pursue informed choices. Organization An embraced information examination as an amazing asset to acquire experiences into client conduct and market patterns. By breaking down information gathered through the CRM framework, the organization had the option to distinguish arising potential open doors and dangers, permitting them to adjust rapidly to changing economic situations. Deals anticipated turned out to be more exact, as authentic information and continuous experiences were utilized to foresee future deals patterns. This assisted in asset allotment as well as in stock administration and supply with binding advancement. Subsequently, Organization A saw a decrease in pointless uses and an expansion in by and large benefit.

Further developed Consumer loyalty

The expanding influence of Organization A's CRM change was expanded consumer loyalty. By understanding their clients better and tending to their requirements all the more, the organization had the option to encourage more grounded and steadfast client connections. With mechanized subsequent meet-ups and customized communications, clients felt esteemed and heard, which thus prompted higher consistency standards and expanded references.

Additionally, the CRM framework worked with an effective issue goal. Client grievances and administration demands were logged and followed, guaranteeing that they were tended to speedily. This prompted less client accelerations and a general improvement in the brand's standing.

Quantifiable Outcomes

The change of deals tasks through CRM at Organization A yielded quantifiable outcomes. The organization revealed a critical expansion in both income and overall revenues. Deals expanded by 20% in the primary year of CRM execution, and this development pattern went on over ensuing years.

Besides, the expense of deals diminished because of expanded proficiency, while client securing costs diminished because of more powerful focusing on and higher client maintenance. The profit from interest in CRM was obvious, and Organization An understood that the underlying interest in innovation and preparation had been taken care of many times over.

Organization An's excursion to change its deals tasks with CRM fills in as a convincing contextual analysis for organizations in different areas. The execution of CRM innovation, joined with a client driven approach and information driven direction, has prompted a surprising improvement in deals execution and consumer loyalty. It shows the capability of CRM as a mechanical arrangement as well as an essential change in the manner organizations draw in with their clients and deal with their deals tasks. In the present high speed and serious business world, embracing CRM might be the way to opening deals development and long haul achievement.

Company B: CRM Strategies for Small Businesses

Client Relationship The board (CRM) is a key part of current business tasks, and it's not only held for huge organizations. Independent ventures, similar to Organization B, can benefit enormously from compelling CRM procedures. In the present quick moving and exceptionally cutthroat market, figuring out your clients and keeping up major areas of strength with them is fundamental for economical development. We should dig into the universe of CRM systems and perceive how Organization B can use them for its potential benefit.

Grasping CRM

CRM includes overseeing and examining client communications all through their lifecycle with an organization. It envelops different cycles, innovations, and methodologies that empower organizations to fabricate enduring associations with their clients. For independent ventures like Organization B, executing CRM can prompt higher consumer loyalty, expanded deals, and further developed client maintenance.

Information is Best

One of the foundations of a powerful CRM is information on the board. Independent ventures should gather, store, and investigate client information to acquire experiences into client conduct and inclinations. This information can incorporate contact data, buy history, and, surprisingly, virtual entertainment connections. Organization B can utilize this data to customize advertising endeavors and proposition fitted answers for individual clients.

Smoothed out Correspondence

A CRM framework can assist Organization B smooth out correspondence with clients. For example, robotized email missions can be set up to send customized messages to clients in light of their past connections and inclinations. This recoveries time as well as guarantees that clients get important data, causing them to feel esteemed.

Client Division

Private companies ought to portion their clients in view of different standards like socioeconomics, buy history, and purchasing recurrence. Thus, Organization B can target explicit client bunches with customized advancements and offers. This designated approach can prompt higher transformation rates and client commitment.

Lead The executives

Proficient leadership is crucial for private ventures. Organization B can utilize CRM to follow leads, sustain possible clients, and convert them into paying clients. A CRM framework can computerize lead scoring and help outreach groups focus on drives that are probably going to change over, eventually further developing the deals interaction.

Client care

Giving great client care is a vital part of CRM. Organization B can utilize CRM devices to follow client requests, protests, and input. This information can assist with distinguishing regions where client care can be improved, prompting higher consumer loyalty and dependability.

Reconciliation of Online Entertainment

In the present computerized age, virtual entertainment assumes a huge part in client communications. Organization B can coordinate online entertainment stages into its CRM procedure to screen client feeling, answer questions, and draw in with clients progressively. This can improve the organization's internet based standing and fabricate trust among clients.

Estimating Achievement

Estimating the outcome of CRM techniques is fundamental. Key execution markers (KPIs) like client degree of consistency, client lifetime worth, and change rates can assist with company B survey the effect of its CRM endeavors. By routinely examining these measurements, the business can calibrate its CRM system for improved results.

Picking the Right CRM Situation

For independent companies, choosing the right CRM situation is urgent. Organization B ought to consider factors like reasonableness, versatility, usability, and reconciliation capacities. Cloud-based CRM arrangements are much of the time a solid match for independent ventures as they offer adaptability and cost-viability.

Preparing and Worker Purchase In

Carrying out a CRM framework ought to be joined by legitimate preparation for representatives. It's fundamental to guarantee that all colleagues comprehend how to really utilize the CRM framework. Their up front investment and dynamic support in the CRM procedure are significant for its prosperity.

Building Trust and Steadfastness

Compelling CRM systems can assist with company B to construct trust and reliability among its client base. At the point when clients feel comprehended, esteemed, and upheld, they are bound to return and prescribe the business to other people. This informal promotion can be a strong resource for independent companies.

Taking everything into account, CRM techniques are not restricted to enormous enterprises; they are similarly fundamental for independent ventures like Organization B. By carrying out viable CRM techniques, private companies can comprehend their clients better, smooth out correspondence, give extraordinary client assistance, and at last drive development and achievement. While the CRM scene might appear to be overpowering, a beneficial speculation can prompt enduring client connections and expanded productivity for organizations, everything being equal.

Company C: CRM in E-commerce

Figuring out Organization C

Organization C is a made up online business organization that works in the shopper hardware industry. With a different scope of items, from cell phones and workstations to shrewd home gadgets and frills, Organization C has effectively explored the advanced scene to cut a specialty for itself. Nonetheless, it provokes normal web based business, including furious contests, quickly developing client assumptions, and the need to adjust to arising innovations.

CRM as the Main impetus

To remain on the ball, Organization C perceived the meaning of CRM. CRM, generally, is a methodology that uses innovation to oversee and examine client cooperations all through the client lifecycle. It envelops innovation as well as a client driven way of thinking that saturates the whole association. Organization C's CRM venture started with the execution of hearty CRM programming, which permitted them to exhaustively catch and examine client information.

Information Driven Navigation

Organization C comprehended the significance of information driven dynamic in the web based business domain. By utilizing CRM information, they acquired experiences into client inclinations, conduct, and buy history. This data was essential in making customized showcasing efforts, item proposals, and designated advancements. CRM apparatuses empowered Organization C to section its client base really, guaranteeing that each portion got custom fitted substance and offers.

Further developed Client care

One of the center principles of CRM is giving extraordinary client assistance.

Organization C executed a multichannel emotionally supportive network that permitted clients to connect through different stages, including email, visit, and web-based entertainment. CRM devices assisted specialists with getting to nitty gritty client profiles, empowering them to resolve gives all the more productively and with an individual touch. The outcome was further developed consumer loyalty and dependability.

Improved Client Commitment

Organization C went past tending to client issues responsively; they proactively drew in with their clients. Robotized CRM work processes permitted them to send follow-up messages, demand criticism, and keep clients informed about new items and advancements. The outcome was more connected with the client base that felt esteemed and heard.

Smoothed out Deals Cycles

CRM additionally smoothed out the deals interaction for Organization C. Their outreach group approached continuous information on client associations, assisting them with understanding where every client was in the purchasing venture.

This took into consideration more compelling lead supporting and transformation. Moreover, CRM programming coordinated consistently with the web based business stage, giving a smooth and durable shopping experience for clients.

Information Security and Protection

In the time of information breaks and expanding worries over security, Organization C comprehended the need to defend client information. They guaranteed that their CRM framework had vigorous safety efforts set up to safeguard delicate client data. This ingrained trust as well as assisted Organization C with following information insurance guidelines.

Estimating Achievement

Organization C knew that executing CRM was a significant speculation, and they expected to gauge the profit from that venture. Through CRM examination, they could follow key execution pointers, for example, client consistency standards, change rates, and client lifetime esteem.

These measurements uncovered the unmistakable advantages of their CRM endeavors, and they reliably saw development here.

Adjusting to Change

The internet business scene is dynamic, with new advancements and patterns continually arising. Organization C stayed deft in its way to deal with CRM, adjusting to changes in client conduct and market patterns. They utilized CRM information to recognize shifts in client inclinations and change their item contributions and advertising systems likewise.

Difficulties and Examples Learned

Organization C's excursion with CRM was not without its difficulties. They confronted issues like information quality, preparing staff on CRM frameworks, and the requirement for steady programming refreshes. In any case, they gained from these difficulties and constantly further developed their CRM system.

The Eventual fate of CRM at Organization C

Looking forward, Organization C considers CRM to be an essential piece of its future development. They are investigating the utilization of computerized reasoning and AI to additionally customize client encounters. They are additionally considering the incorporation of expanded reality and augmented reality advances to upgrade the web based shopping experience.

All in all, Organization C's fruitful execution of CRM in web based business exhibits the groundbreaking force of client relationship with the board.

By saddling information driven navigation, upgrading client assistance, and smoothing out deals processes, Organization C has solidified its situation as a forerunner in the online business industry. As they keep on adjusting to changing business sector elements, the fate of CRM at Organization C holds invigorating opportunities for much more prominent client commitment and fulfillment.

Chapter 7
Future Trends in CRM

Man-made brainpower and AI: Man-made intelligence and ML are ready to reform CRM. They will empower organizations to investigate tremendous measures of information to make forecasts, robotize routine assignments, and customize client encounters. Chatbots and menial helpers fueled by simulated intelligence are turning out to be progressively well known for dealing with client requests continuously.

Hyper-Personalization: Clients are anticipating more customized encounters. Future CRM frameworks will utilize information from different sources, including virtual entertainment and online way of behaving, to make exceptionally individualized client ventures. This degree of personalization can improve client unwaveringly and drive deals.

Omnichannel Incorporation: CRM stages are getting towards consistent incorporation across all correspondence channels, like email, talk, online entertainment, and telephone. This guarantees that client information and corporations are predictable across channels, giving a bound together and helpful experience.

Information Protection and Security: With expanding worries over information protection, CRM frameworks should adjust to stricter guidelines. Future patterns incorporate high level encryption, information anonymization, and more prominent straightforwardness in how client information is utilized and secured.

IoT Coordination: The Web of Things (IoT) is setting out open doors for CRM by empowering the assortment of constant information from associated gadgets. CRM will utilize this information to give proactive client assistance and gain experiences into client conduct.

128

Voice Innovation: Voice-actuated menial helpers and shrewd speakers are turning out to be more predominant. CRM frameworks are incorporating voice innovation to offer voice-initiated orders for overseeing client associations and acquiring bits of knowledge from voice information.

Blockchain for Client Information Security: Blockchain innovation can improve the security of client information, forestalling information breaks and unapproved access. It can likewise furnish clients with more command over their information, giving or denying access on a case by case basis.

Prescient Investigation: CRM frameworks will progressively utilize prescient examination to conjecture client conduct, for example, purchasing behaviors, beat rates, and client inclinations. This assists organizations with settling on informed choices and designing their systems appropriately.

Client Self-Administration: Self-administration choices will extend, empowering clients to determine issues and track down data all alone. Chatbots, information bases, and intelligent FAQs will turn out to be more modern, decreasing the requirement for human client care.

Social CRM: The impact of web-based entertainment on CRM is developing. Organizations will progressively utilize social CRM to screen online entertainment channels, draw in with clients, and gain bits of knowledge into feeling and patterns.

Increased and Computer generated Reality: These advancements can change the client experience. For example, AR can empower clients to picture items in their own current circumstance, while VR can make vivid shopping encounters. CRM will assume a part in overseeing and customizing these encounters.

Client Excursion Planning: Understanding the client excursion will be fundamental in CRM. Progressed examination will assist with planning client collaborations, distinguish trouble spots, and streamline touchpoints to make a smoother and seriously fulfilling venture.

Membership Based Models: Numerous organizations are moving towards membership based models. CRM should adjust to oversee repeating charging, client maintenance, and conveying esteem over the long haul.

Voice of the Client (VoC) Investigation: Organizations will focus harder on VoC information, gathering and examining criticism from clients to make information driven enhancements to items and administrations.

Maintainability and CSR Combination: Organizations are progressively coordinating supportability and corporate social obligation (CSR) into their business techniques. CRM will help in following and conveying these endeavors to clients, building trust and reliability.

All in all, the fate of CRM is extraordinarily energizing. With artificial intelligence, personalization, information security, and an accentuation on client experience, organizations will be better prepared to comprehend and serve their clients. Be that as it may, it's essential to stay versatile, as the CRM scene is consistently developing, answering changing client needs and innovative progressions.

AI and Machine Learning in CRM

Client Relationship The executives (CRM) has been an urgent part of business tasks for a really long time. It includes the systems and advancements that organizations use to oversee and break down client communications all through the client lifecycle. Lately, the reconciliation of Man-made consciousness (simulated intelligence) and AI (ML) into CRM frameworks has upset how organizations draw in with their clients. This combination of advances has enabled organizations to customize their connections, upgrade client assistance, and drive functional effectiveness in manners that were beforehand impossible.

Simulated intelligence and ML: A Short Outline

Prior to plunging into the effect of simulated intelligence and ML in CRM, it's fundamental to comprehend what these terms envelop. Man-made intelligence alludes to the advancement of PC frameworks that can perform errands that normally require human insight. This incorporates getting the hang of, thinking, critical thinking, and independent direction. Then again, ML is a subset of man-made intelligence that spotlights the improvement of calculations and factual models that empower frameworks to gain and improve from information without being unequivocally customized. In CRM, these advancements can be bridled to dissect client information, robotize undertakings, and anticipate client conduct.

Customized Client Encounters

One of the main benefits of coordinating man-made intelligence and ML into CRM is the capacity to convey profoundly customized client encounters. Overwhelmingly, these frameworks can recognize patterns and examples in client conduct. For example, they can section clients in view of their inclinations, buy history, and online way of behaving. This empowers organizations to tailor promoting messages, offers, and item proposals to individual clients, improving the probability of making a deal and further developing consumer loyalty.

Chatbots and Menial helpers

Chatbots and menial helpers have become progressively normal in CRM. These man-made intelligence controlled instruments can deal with client requests, offer help, and help with different assignments. They are accessible all day, every day, which is a huge benefit for organizations as they can propose nonstop client care without causing extra work costs. Chatbots and remote helpers can determine straightforward client issues, direct clients to the right office, and even cycle orders, all progressively.

Prescient Examination

Artificial intelligence and ML likewise empower organizations to tackle the force of prescient examination in CRM. Prescient examination utilizes authentic information and calculations to conjecture future patterns and occasions. In CRM, this is especially important for anticipating client conduct. For instance, it can guess when a client is probably going to really make a buy, empowering organizations to time their showcasing endeavors. It can likewise help in recognizing clients who may be in danger of agitation, permitting organizations to go to proactive lengths to hold them.

Mechanization of Routine Errands

CRM frameworks customarily require manual information passage, which can be tedious and mistake inclined. Computer based intelligence and ML innovations can robotize these normal errands, lessening the responsibility on human representatives and limiting blunders. For example, information can be naturally caught from email connections, virtual entertainment, and different sources, and afterward incorporated into the CRM framework. This recoveries time as well as guarantees that client information is dependably cutting-edge and exact.

Productive Lead Scoring

In deals and promoting, lead scoring is a basic cycle. It includes doling out values to leads in view of their probability to change over into clients. Simulated intelligence and ML can extraordinarily improve lead scoring by examining information to distinguish which leads are probably going to bring about a deal. This permits deals and showcasing groups to focus on their endeavors on the most encouraging leads, expanding change rates and further developing productivity.

Further developed Client assistance

Client assistance is a vital piece of CRM, and simulated intelligence and ML have reformed this viewpoint. Computer based intelligence controlled chatbots, for instance, can deal with an extensive variety of client requests, opening up human specialists to deal with additional perplexing issues. Furthermore, man-made intelligence can examine client feeling by observing online entertainment and different channels, empowering organizations to proactively address client concerns and issues.

Information Driven Bits of knowledge

Artificial intelligence and ML engage organizations to remove important bits of knowledge from their CRM information. These advancements can dissect immense datasets and reveal patterns, relationships, and open doors that may be unimaginable for people to physically recognize. Organizations can utilize these experiences to go with information driven choices, advance their procedures, and remain in front of their rivals.

Difficulties and Contemplations

While the coordination of computer based intelligence and ML in CRM offers various advantages, it's not without its difficulties. Organizations should address worries about information protection and security, as the utilization of man-made intelligence frequently includes gathering and dissecting delicate client data. Furthermore, there is an expectation to learn and adapt for carrying out these innovations really. Organizations need to put resources into preparing their workers and guaranteeing the computer based intelligence and ML calculations are adjusted for their particular requirements.

Taking everything into account

The mix of computer based intelligence and ML into CRM frameworks has achieved a change in the manner organizations draw in with their clients. Customized encounters, computerization of routine errands, prescient examination, and productive lead scoring are only a portion of the benefits that artificial intelligence and ML offer in the domain of CRM. As organizations keep on saddling the force of these advancements, they will be better prepared to fabricate enduring and productive associations with their clients, eventually driving their progress in an undeniably serious commercial center.

Omni-Channel Customer Engagement

In the present hyperconnected world, the outcome of a business is complicatedly attached to its capacity to really connect with clients. With the appearance of the web, online entertainment, and cell phones, clients currently have numerous touchpoints through which they cooperate with organizations. This shift has led to the idea of omni-channel client commitment, which includes flawlessly coordinating different channels to make a brought together and steady client experience. In this article, we will investigate the importance, advantages, and difficulties of omni-channel client commitment.

Figuring out Omni-Channel Client Commitment

Omni-channel client commitment is an essential methodology that recognizes the different manners by which clients cooperate with organizations. This approach incorporates both physical and advanced channels, including physical stores, sites, online entertainment, portable applications, email, from there, the sky's the limit. The objective is to guarantee that clients get a predictable and consistent experience no matter what the channel they decide for their connection.

At the core of omni-channel commitment is the idea of "channel free-thought." This implies that organizations don't focus on one channel over another but instead center around giving a brought together, firm insight across all channels. For example, in the event that a client adds a thing to their web based shopping basket however chooses to visit the actual store, they ought to have the option to get their truck available and complete the purchase with next to no problem.

The Meaning of Omni-Channel Commitment

Client Driven Approach: Omni-channel commitment is in a general sense client driven. It perceives that the client, not the channel, ought to be at the focal point of the business technique. This approach is lined up with the advanced purchaser's assumption for customized and advantageous encounters.

Consistency: Consistency across channels is indispensable. Clients expect a similar degree of administration and data whether they are perusing a site, visiting via web-based entertainment, or conversing with a client care delegate. Irregularities can prompt dissatisfaction and, at last, loss of business.

Expanded Deals: A consistent omni-divert experience can bring about expanded deals. At the point when clients can undoubtedly switch between channels to make buys or get data, they are bound to finish exchanges. This can prompt higher transformation rates and client faithfulness.

Information Driven Experiences: An omni-channel approach creates an abundance of information that can be saddled to figure out client conduct, inclinations, and patterns. This information driven approach permits organizations to go with informed choices and refine their methodologies.

Upper hand: Organizations that effectively carry out omni-channel commitment gain an upper hand. They hang out in the market since they give a prevalent client experience. This can be a huge differentiator in a jam-packed commercial center.

Advantages of Omni-Channel Commitment

Further developed Client Experience: One of the essential advantages of omni-channel client commitment is the improvement of the general client experience. At the point when clients can undoubtedly get to data, make buys, and get support across different channels, they feel esteemed and fulfilled.

Improved Client Reliability: Fulfilled clients are bound to become steadfast clients. They are additionally bound to prescribe your image to other people. Omni-channel commitment fabricates trust and fortifies client connections, which, thus, drives steadfastness.

Effectiveness and Cost Reserve funds: While executing an omni-channel methodology might require an underlying speculation, it can prompt expense reserve funds over the long haul. Smoothed out cycles and better information use can prompt diminished functional expenses.

Information Driven Navigation: The information produced from omni-channel associations gives significant experiences. Organizations can utilize this information to tailor their advertising efforts, further develop item contributions, and settle on informed choices in regards to stock, staffing, and other functional viewpoints.

Upper hand: In a serious business scene, offering an unrivaled omni-channel experience can separate your business from rivals. Clients are bound to pick a brand that gives comfort and consistency.

Difficulties of Omni-Channel Commitment

Complex Execution: Omni-channel procedures can be intricate to execute. Incorporating different frameworks and guaranteeing a consistent information stream can be testing, particularly for enormous associations with numerous touchpoints.

Information Security: Taking care of client information across different channels requires rigid safety efforts to safeguard delicate data. The gamble of information breaks is a critical worry in omni-channel commitment.

Asset Serious: Executing and keeping an omni-channel technique requests critical assets, including monetary ventures, staff preparing, and progressing specialized help.

Protection from Change: Representatives might oppose changes in their jobs and obligations that accompany executing an omni-channel system. It's significant to deal with this opposition and give sufficient preparation and backing.

Consistency Across Channels: Keeping a steady encounter across channels can be challenging. Each channel has its exceptional elements and limits, making it hard to guarantee a uniform client experience.

All in all, omni-channel client commitment is in excess of a pattern; it's a key change in how organizations and clients connect. It offers various advantages, including further developed client experience, improved unwaveringly, and an upper hand. Be that as it may, it likewise presents difficulties connected with execution, information security, and consistency. To prevail in this time, organizations should embrace the omni-channel approach, adjust to changing client assumptions, and influence the tremendous measures of information it produces to remain ahead in a quickly developing business sector.

Voice and Chatbot Integration

In the present high speed computerized world, organizations are continually looking for creative ways of further developing client care and smooth out correspondence. The joining of voice innovation and chatbots is a great representation of how organizations are adjusting to address these issues. Voice and chatbot mix offers a harmonious relationship that can improve client encounters, increment proficiency, and eventually drive business development.

Voice innovation has seen a brilliant ascent in fame over the course of the last ten years. Shrewd speakers, remote helpers, and voice-enacted gadgets have become omnipresent in families and working environments. Simultaneously, chatbots have additionally become fundamental apparatuses for client care and data recovery on sites and informing stages. Joining these two advances opens up a plenty of potential outcomes, permitting organizations to connect with clients in a more normal and productive manner.

One of the essential benefits of incorporating voice and chatbots is the capacity to give a consistent multi-channel insight. Clients today hope to cooperate with organizations based on their conditions, whether through voice orders, text visits, or a mix of both. By consolidating these two innovations, organizations can take special care of a more extensive crowd, upgrading openness and inclusivity. For example, a client can begin a discussion with a chatbot on a site and afterward consistently change to voice collaboration when they move to a shrewd speaker, all while keeping up with setting and consistency in their communications.

In addition, voice and chatbot reconciliation can essentially further develop client service. Chatbots are superb for taking care of routine requests and errands, for example, giving item data, request following, or responding to regularly got clarification on some pressing issues. In any case, there are occurrences where a more customized and human touch is required. Voice innovation can be flawlessly incorporated when chatbots arrive at their restrictions, permitting a client to talk straightforwardly with a human specialist or get more intricate help. This guarantees that clients get the right degree of help, streamlining the client support insight.

Cost-productivity is one more convincing justification for incorporating voice and chatbots. While chatbots handle monotonous and direct errands productively, voice innovation can upgrade robotization significantly further. For example, organizations can convey voice-initiated IVR (Intuitive Voice Reaction) frameworks to deal with an extensive variety of client requests, decreasing the responsibility on human specialists and saving time and assets. This mix of chatbots and voice robotization prompts massive expense reserve funds for organizations, as it permits them to scale their client care tasks without causing corresponding expansions in labor costs.

The idea of conversational computer based intelligence is at the core of this incorporation. It includes preparing chatbots to comprehend and answer normal language and discourse, causing communications with clients to feel more human-like. This capacity is especially important in voice interfaces, where clients anticipate a conversational encounter. With progressions in normal language handling (NLP) and discourse acknowledgment, chatbots can decipher and answer voice orders precisely, giving a smoother and more natural client experience.

Personalization is one more region where voice and chatbot mix can sparkle. With the consolidated abilities of these advancements, organizations can assemble and break down client information from both text and voice connections. This information can be utilized to make customized proposals, offers, and content. For example, a client's past chatbot communications can illuminate a voice colleague about their inclinations and requirements, permitting it to give custom-made help. This personalization improves the client experience as well as lifts client commitment and dedication.

Security and protection are basic worries in the computerized age. Voice and chatbot coordination requires vigorous safety efforts to safeguard delicate client data. This incorporates encryption, secure verification, and consistency with information assurance guidelines. As organizations progressively influence voice and chatbot innovation, guaranteeing the wellbeing of client information is principal. Organizations that effectively explore this challenge can construct entrust with their clients, upgrading their standing and believability.

Consolidating voice and chatbot combination likewise opens entryways for creative advertising procedures. Organizations can utilize voice connection points to convey advancements, promotions, and content straightforwardly to clients. For instance, a client collaborating with a voice-enacted collaborator could get customized item suggestions or select offers. This immediate and intelligent methodology can be exceptionally viable in driving deals and client commitment.

Moreover, voice and chatbot mix can upset availability for individuals with incapacities. Voice innovation is a distinct advantage for people with visual hindrances, making computerized corporations more comprehensive. By incorporating voice and chatbots, organizations can guarantee that their items and administrations are open to a more extensive crowd, improving their social obligation and market reach.

All in all, the mix of voice and chatbots addresses a convincing collaboration that offers various advantages to organizations and clients the same. This cooperative relationship smoothes out correspondence, further develops client assistance, improves proficiency, and drives cost investment funds. Additionally, it prepares for creative promoting systems, personalization, and availability enhancements. As innovation keeps on propelling, the opportunities for voice and chatbot reconciliation are boundless, and organizations that embrace this joining are strategically situated to flourish in the advanced age.

Customer-Centric Approaches

In the present savagely cutthroat business scene, the progress of an organization generally relies upon its capacity to fulfill and hold clients. This idea is at the core of what is known as a client driven approach. The thought behind this approach is straightforward yet extraordinary: put the client at the focal point of each and every choice, technique, and communication. In this 700-word investigation, we will dig into the standards, advantages, and difficulties of embracing client driven approaches in business.

Standards of Client Centricity

Understanding Client Needs: The foundation of a client driven approach is figuring out the necessities and inclinations of your clients. This expects top to bottom statistical surveying, information investigation, and a compassionate comprehension of the client's excursion. By appreciating their cravings and trouble spots, organizations can fit items and administrations to meet or surpass their assumptions.

Personalization: No two clients are something very similar. Perceiving this, client driven organizations customize their connections. This might include making custom-made promoting efforts, giving redid item suggestions, or in any event, offering one-on-one help. The objective is to cause clients to feel esteemed and comprehended.

Consistent Client Experience: Consistency is vital. A client driven approach endeavors to give a consistent encounter across all touchpoints. Whether a client communicates with your image through your site, web-based entertainment, coming up, or by means of client support, the experience ought to be rational and charming.

Tuning in and Criticism: Organizations that focus on their clients effectively look for input and are available to analysis. This data is priceless in making enhancements. Paying attention to clients can prompt item upgrades, process streamlining, and at last, expanded client dependability.

Worker Commitment: Your representatives are your image diplomats. A client driven approach includes connecting with and preparing your staff to focus on consumer loyalty. Blissful and thoroughly prepared representatives are bound to convey brilliant assistance.

Advantages of Client Driven Approaches

Upgraded Client Dependability: By reliably addressing client needs and customizing cooperations, organizations assemble solid connections that lead to expanded client unwaveringly. Fulfilled clients are bound to return and become advocates for your image.

Expanded Income: Cheerful, steadfast clients are bound to spend more, and they frequently become recurrent purchasers. This outcomes in expanded income and long haul productivity.

Diminished Client Agitate: A client driven approach can essentially decrease client stir. Clients are less inclined to change to a contender in the event that they feel esteemed and their requirements are met reliably.

Further developed Brand Notoriety: Informal exchange is a strong promoting device. Fulfilled clients are bound to prescribe your image to other people, upgrading your standing and drawing in new clients.

Upper hand: In a market where most organizations are client driven, embracing this approach can separate your organization. A significant differentiator can give you an upper hand.

Difficulties of Carrying out Client Driven Approaches

Protection from Change: Moving to a client driven approach might require huge changes in organization culture and cycles. Opposition from representatives who are familiar with an alternate approach to working can be a test.

Information The executives: To get it and customize the client experience, organizations need admittance to immense measures of information. Overseeing and using this information really can be a mind boggling undertaking, and information protection concerns should be tended to.

Cost and Asset Allotment: Focusing on the client experience can be exorbitant. Assets might should be diverted from different region of the business to put resources into client driven drives.

Consistency Across Channels: Giving a consistent encounter across different client touchpoints can challenge. Guaranteeing predictable marking, informing, and nature of administration requires cautious coordination.

Overpersonalization: While personalization is a vital component of client centricity, there's a scarcely discernible difference between offering some benefit and being nosy. Overpersonalization can make clients anxious and hurt the client experience.

All in all, taking on a client driven approach isn't simply a pattern yet a key change in how organizations work. A methodology focuses on understanding and addressing client needs, and it accompanies a large group of advantages, including expanded client faithfulness, income, and a solid brand notoriety. Be that as it may, it's not without its difficulties, for example, protection from change, information the executives, and the allotment of assets.

During a time where clients have more options than any other time, organizations that place the client at the focal point of their methodology are better prepared to flourish. Whether you are a little startup or an enormous partnership, the way to progress progressively goes through the core of your clients. Embracing client driven approaches can be the way to opening supported development and long haul productivity in the present unique business scene.

CONCLUSION

The Role of CRM in Maximizing Sales Final Thoughts References and Additional Resources

In the present profoundly aggressive business scene, the meaning of Client Relationship The executives (CRM) in boosting deals couldn't possibly be more significant. It has developed from being a simple programming instrument to an essential basic for organizations across different enterprises. This article has dug into the complex parts of CRM, its critical job in improving deals, and the manners in which it engages associations to develop and keep up areas of strength with connections.

CRM frameworks have changed the manner in which organizations connect with clients. They give a concentrated stage to gathering, putting away, and dissecting client information, which permits associations to acquire important experiences into client conduct and inclinations. This, thus, works with more customized and designated showcasing and deals endeavors.

One of the essential advantages of CRM is its capacity to expand effectiveness and efficiency in outreach groups. Through mechanization and smoothed out processes, agents can zero in more on drawing in with clients and shutting bargains. CRM likewise helps with lead the board, guaranteeing that outreach groups focus on their endeavors on the most encouraging possibilities.

Moreover, CRM empowers organizations to sustain long haul client connections. By keeping a thorough record of client connections, organizations can give a more customized and mindful help. This improves consumer loyalty as well as cultivates client faithfulness, prompting rehash business and references.

Additionally, CRM frameworks enable associations to settle on information driven choices. Through the examination of client information, organizations can distinguish patterns, inclinations, and potential open doors. This understanding is significant for thinking up viable deals techniques and item advancement drives that resound with the interest group.

As innovation keeps on progressing, CRM frameworks are turning out to be progressively refined. Man-made brainpower and AI are being coordinated into CRM programming, considering prescient investigation and, surprisingly, more customized client encounters. This pattern is supposed to additionally change deals and showcasing rehearses before very long.

CRM assumes a significant part in boosting deals by upgrading client connections, further developing outreach group productivity, and giving important bits of knowledge through information examination. It is at this point not an extravagance however a need for organizations planning to flourish in a serious market. In any case, it's a memorable fundamental that carrying out CRM is certainly not a one-time exertion; it requires progressing responsibility and transformation to meet the constantly developing necessities of clients and the business climate.

Extra Assets:

HubSpot CRM - An exhaustive CRM stage with different instruments to help deals and client connections.

Salesforce - Gives an itemized outline of CRM and its importance for private companies.

Gartner CRM Exploration - Access inside and out examination and reports on CRM patterns and advancements.

LinkedIn Learning - CRM Courses - An assortment of courses to improve how you might interpret CRM and its applications.

Forrester CRM Reports - Investigate CRM-related research reports from Forrester, a famous examination association.

These assets can give further experiences into CRM and its part in deals, guaranteeing you stay all around educated about this significant perspective regarding present day business.